QUICK AND EASY
SOY AND TOFU RECIPES

Polly Grimaldi

Bristol Publishing Enterprises
Hayward, California

A **nitty gritty**® Cookbook

Printed in the United States of America.

ISBN: 1-55867-292-3

Cover design: Frank J. Paredes
Cover photography: John A. Benson
Food stylist: Susan Devaty
Illustrator: Shanti Nelson

CONTENTS

This book is dedicated to my husband John, whose diligent efforts at the computer contributed to making it possible.

Janice Cole, Cathy Raphael, Melanie Rapp, Vitaly and Nadya Semenchenko, Jeanette Wurster—Thank you!

To Kevin Titter who has the unique quality of taking another's dream and giving it as much loving assistance as though it were his own . . . . Thank you, Kevin.

AN INTRODUCTION TO SOY AND TOFU

Writing this book was never work. Instead it offered me endless hours of exploration and creativity. It all began when the Delaware Soybean Board asked me to represent them at the State Fair, and I began to research this incredible little bean.

SOY AND TOFU BACKGROUND

Tofu originated in China over 2,000 years ago. Today it is one of the most popular foods for China's 800 (or so) million people. Every Chinese province makes its own variety of tofu and has its own name and pronunciation for its own product. In Japan, tofu-making contests are held each year in which master craftsmen are judged on the texture, flavor and appearance of their tofu, as well as the accuracy and speed of their cutting. Tofu is as much a part of Asian culture, language and cooking as bread is for the western world. In America, the average annual consumption of bread is 73 loaves per person. In Japan, the average annual consumption of tofu is 70 twelve-ounce cakes per year, and much higher than that in China and Taiwan.

HEALTH BENEFITS OF SOY

Soy is associated with many health benefits, including reduced risk of breast cancer (and other cancers), heart disease, osteoporosis, diabetes, tinnitus and kidney problems. Soy isoflavones are increasingly being considered a viable alternative to hormone replacement therapy (HRT), particularly since soy doesn't have the risks of HRT. It has the benefits of relieving the hot flashes of menopause while at the same time lowering cholesterol, helping to prevent osteoporosis, and possibly increasing bone density.

Isoflavones are found in only a handful of plants, including soy. Their primary function is as an antioxidant, a powerful chemical scavenger that can neutralize damaging free radicals.

The protein in soy is just about equivalent to the protein in meat, dairy and eggs. It is slightly low in the amino acid methionine, a deficit that can be made up by serving grain-based foods (such as rice, pasta or bread) with soy.

Vitamin B12 is one of the vitamins most often deficient in the diets of vegetarians who exclude dairy products as well as meats. Recent research has found that fermented soy foods, miso, sea vegetables and especially tempeh are good sources of vitamin B12.

A diet of soy should be accompanied by foods rich in iodine, such as sea vegetables (seaweeds, or marine algae). A number of studies have suggested a link between heavy soy ingestion and thyroid autoimmune disease or goiter, both in infants on soy formulas and in adults eating a large amount of soy foods.

COOKING SOYBEANS

Dried soybeans should be soaked before cooking. Cover 1 pound of soybeans with 6 to

8 cups of water and soak overnight. Drain the beans and cover with 6 to 8 cups of fresh water. Bring to a boil, reduce the heat, and simmer for about 3 hours, until beans are tender. (Black soybeans will cook in about half the time.) For a speedier soak, cover dried beans with 6 to 8 cups of hot water, boil for 5 minutes, and then soak for 1 hour before cooking. Soybeans, like other beans, will not become tender if you add salt to the cooking water, so season the soybeans after they are cooked.

Canned soybeans are surrounded by a transparent gelatinous substance. This will eventually disappear when the beans are heated. Rinse this material off in a strainer, if beans are to be added to a cold dish such as a salad.

Edamame (ed-ah-MAH-may), or green soybeans, are available in most supermarkets and natural food stores. These are fresh soybeans harvested just prior to maturity. They are sold in the pod or shelled and packed in airtight bags. Refrigerated beans must be used within 2 days. Frozen edamame will keep for several months. To cook edamame, place beans in boiling water, cover and simmer for 10 to 12 minutes, until tender. Serve as a vegetable side dish or add them to salads or soups. Cooked, salted edamame are a great snack to nibble on while watching a movie or ball game.

BUYING, PREPARING AND STORING TOFU

Tofu is made from cooked soybeans with the fiber removed and a coagulant added. It contains all the protein, fat and carbohydrates (other than fiber) of soybeans. Tofu is the ideal diet food. A typical 8-ounce serving contains only 147 calories and supplies the body with 11.5 grams of usable protein.

Tofu can be found in the produce section of the supermarket, and is usually sold in blocks packed in water. It will last for 5 weeks in the refrigerator or 6 months in the freezer. Once opened, refrigerated tofu must have its water changed daily. There is also a boxed tofu available in health food stores, co-ops and some supermarkets that does not require refrigeration and has a shelf life of several months until opened. Dried frozen tofu is sold in small paper boxes as dried bean curd.

To measure fresh tofu, pour off the liquid and pat the block well with paper towels. Crumble or chop into chunks, place in your measuring cup and press to fill to the desired measurement.

SILKEN AND FIRM TOFU

Tofu comes in a variety of firmness, determined by the amount of water it retains. Silken tofu is soft—best suited for dips, sauces, beverages, etc. Mash or puree tofu in your food processor or blender, and use in place of sour cream or mayonnaise. Medium tofu works for almost all dishes. Firm tofu is best for chopping into cubes, julienned, in stir-fries, etc., and is a good substitute for ricotta or cream cheese in recipes.

There are now several forms of processed tofu available in the United States. Deep fried tofu cutlets are whole cakes of tofu that have been pressed and deep fried until golden brown. Deep fried tofu burgers are tofu and vegetable patties that look like large hamburgers. Deep fried tofu pouches are thin pouches that can be stuffed with any filling. All are high in protein.

BUYING, PREPARING AND STORING TEMPEH

To make tempeh, soybeans are fermented with a grain such as rice or millet. A "starter" such as tempeh from a previous batch is added to begin the fermentation process. The result is a tender, chewy cake of soybeans with a smoky or nutty flavor similar to that of mushrooms. Tempeh can be purchased at local supermarkets or natural food stores in the frozen food section. Tempeh keeps well in the freezer for several months. If refrigerated it will keep for about 10 days. If it develops mold on the surface (it is similar to cheese in this regard) simply scrape it off, as it is harmless.

Tempeh can be steamed, marinated, sautéed, grilled or broiled. You can crumble it into pasta sauces, chili or soups.

SOY FLOUR

Soy flour is made from roasted soybeans that have been ground into a fine powder. It is a source of high-quality protein and other nutrients. Two kinds of soy flour are available: natural or full-fat soy flour, which contains the natural oils found in the soybean, and defatted soy flour, in which the oils have been removed during processing.

- Soy flour can be used as-is or it can be lightly toasted first to enhance its nutty flavor. Simply cook in a dry skillet over moderate heat, stirring occasionally, until lightly browned.

- A small amount of soy flour added to regular flour increases the nutritional value of a loaf of bread. When adding soy flour to a bread recipe, place 2 tablespoons of soy flour in a 1-cup measuring cup before adding the wheat flour. Always stir soy flour before measuring, since it is easily compacted.

- You can substitute up to a quarter of the total flour called for, in recipes for baked products that are not yeast-raised. Soy flour is free of gluten (gluten holds bread together), so it cannot replace all the wheat flour. Baked products containing soy flour tend to brown more quickly; it may be necessary to shorten the baking time or lower the temperature.

- One tablespoon of full-fat soy flour mixed with 1 tablespoon water can replace an egg in a recipe. Baked goods made with tofu or soy flour retain their moisture. In fact, they become even moister the day after baking. It is a good idea to freeze soy-baked goods if they are not used within 2 to 3 days.

BUYING, USING AND STORING SOYMILK

Soymilk is the rich creamy milk of whole soybeans. With its unique, nutty flavor and high nutrition, soymilk can be used in a variety of ways. In China and Japan, fresh soymilk is made daily using a simple, centuries-old process of grinding soaked and cooked soybeans and pressing the dissolved soymilk out of the beans. In these countries, soymilk is sold by street vendors or in cafes.

Soymilk is sold in supermarkets, health food stores and co-ops. It is most commonly found in aseptic (non-refrigerated) quart and 8-ounce containers, but is also sold refrigerated in plastic quart and half-gallon containers. Unopened, aseptically packaged soymilk can be stored at room temperature for several months. Once it is opened, the soymilk must be refrigerated and will stay fresh for about 5 days. Soymilk is also sold as a powder, which is then mixed with water. Soymilk powder should be stored in the refrigerator or freezer.

Soymilk is available plain or in a variety of flavors including chocolate, vanilla, carob and almond. With the growing interest in lower-fat products, a number of "lite" soymilks, with reduced fat content, are appearing on the market.

Soymilk can be used in almost any way that cow's milk is used. Try plain or flavored soymilk as a refreshing drink. Pour soymilk over hot or cold breakfast cereal. Use soymilk to make cream sauces and cream soups that are cholesterol-free and low in saturated fat. Make rich pancakes and waffles. Create your own delicious shakes with soymilk, ice cream or tofu and fruit. Try soymilk instead of evaporated milk to produce custards and pumpkin pies. Like cow's milk, soymilk will curdle when an acid, such as lemon juice, is added.

SOY OIL

The oil extracted from soybeans is low in saturated fat; is a source of Omega-3 fatty acids (the kind found in fish oil that reduces the risk of heart disease); and has a mild flavor. It is excellent for frying since it doesn't smoke when you cook at high temperatures. It is the oil most frequently used in vegetable oil, and is the most widely used oil in the United States.

MISO

Miso is a rich salty condiment used extensively in Japanese cooking. Miso is made by taking soybeans and a grain such as rice and combining the mixture with salt and a mold culture, then aging it in vats for 3 to 4 years.

Soybean miso contains no grain; it is made exclusively from soybeans. Soybean miso is extremely salty and is used in many recipes as a seasoning.

In Japan, different types of miso are prepared and evaluated much like fine wines and cheeses are judged in the United States. A well-known Japanese proverb states that a bowl of miso soup each day keeps the doctor away, and traditional folk wisdom is laden with sayings about the value of miso as a medicine to cure colds, improve metabolism, clear the skin, aid in digestion and build resistance to parasitic diseases.

Many people on salt-restricted diets might try miso as an alternative. Miso contains only 12% salt yet has a rich pungent flavor. It can impart all the desired taste without the addition of added salt.

Miso soup mix is available in boxed packets at health food stores and food co-ops.

OTHER SOY PRODUCTS

- *Meat analogs* are non-meat foods made from soy protein and other ingredients combined to appear similar to meat. Some are designed to taste like meat, flavored like beef, pork, chicken and even tuna. Others are crafted to be like hot dogs, hamburgers or deli meat. Their nutritional value varies; read the label. However, if made primarily from soybeans, they are rich sources of protein, iron and B vitamins. They are usually found in the specialty or natural foods section of the supermarket. Natural food stores and co-ops have an extensive selection. Meat analogs are used in the same fashion as their meat cousins. Soy-based cold cuts are great in sandwiches; imitation bacon and sausage are cooked in exactly the same way as their meat counterparts.

- *TSP (textured soy protein)* and *TVP (textured vegetable protein)* are made from defatted compressed soy flour. TSP and TVP are sold granulated and in chunks, and must be rehydrated with boiling water or other liquid before using. Rehydrated granular TSP resembles ground beef in texture, and TSP chunks resemble stew meat.

- *Soy sauce* is a dark liquid made from fermented soybeans. It is salty-tasting, but has less sodium than table salt. Shoyu is a soy sauce usually made with the addition of wheat, tamari is a soy-only sauce, and teriyaki is soy sauce flavored with vinegar, sugar and other seasonings.

- *Soy cheese* comes in a number of varieties and can be substituted wherever dairy cheese is used.

- *Yuba* (also called dried bean curd, bean curd sheets, or bean curd skin) is the thin layer formed on the surface of hot soymilk as it cools. It is commonly sold fresh, half dried and dried and is very high in protein.

As you read the recipes in this book you will discover that, using your own imagination, you can create many variations to your liking. Each recipe will become an alternative to fat-laden dishes made with cream, dairy cheese and meats.

It is my vision that this book not only brings you information but that it also brings you hope—hope to live a long, healthy life. With this vision, explore this book, and allow the healing properties of soy to become part of your long, healthy life.

BREAKFAST

TOFU AND SCRAMBLED EGGS

Any of the following are delicious when sautéed with eggs and tofu: chives, crushed garlic, green onions, onions, bean sprouts or alfalfa sprouts. Season with soy sauce.

1 tbs. butter
6 oz. firm tofu
2 eggs, lightly beaten
salt and pepper to taste

Melt butter in a skillet over medium heat. Mash tofu in a bowl and add eggs. Season with salt and pepper. Pour egg-tofu mixture into skillet and scramble until firm.

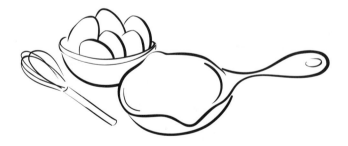

TOFU OMELET WITH MUSHROOMS

Servings: 2–3

The Chinese refer to soy as "the meat without bones" because soy provides 60% of the day's protein in Asian countries. You can fill this omelet with salsa, cheese—or whatever you like.

6 oz. firm tofu, crumbled
3 eggs, lightly beaten
1 tbs. soy sauce
$\frac{1}{2}$ tsp. sugar
2 tbs. sesame seeds or tahini (sesame seed paste)
1 tbs. butter or soy oil
2 onions, chopped
3 large mushrooms, sliced

Combine tofu, eggs, soy sauce, sugar and sesame seeds in a bowl. Mix well. Melt butter in a skillet over medium heat and add onions and mushrooms. Cook for 3 minutes, until onions are transparent. Pour in tofu-egg mixture. Cook until firm.

TOFU POACHED EGG

In both China and Japan the making of tofu is considered an art. One first becomes an apprentice to a master tofu maker much the same as any student in the western world would study under a master craftsman. For the master tofu maker daily practice increases the energy and meaning he puts into his work. Thus the form, taste and quality of tofu in Eastern culture is judged much as we in the West would judge any fine piece of art.

½ pkg. (14 oz. pkg.) firm tofu
½ tsp. soy sauce
½ tsp. lemon juice
1 egg

Scoop a hollow big enough to hold an egg out of the upper surface of tofu. Pour soy sauce and lemon juice into hollow, then crack egg into hollow.

Bring 1 inch of water to a boil over high heat in a saucepan. Carefully add tofu boat. Reduce heat to low, cover and simmer for 3 minutes, or until egg is firm. Scoop out tofu-and-egg boat with a slotted spoon and serve.

ONION BACON QUICHE

This versatile quiche can be served for breakfast, lunch or dinner.

8 slices bacon, chopped
2 cups finely chopped sweet onions
1/2 tsp. caraway seeds
3 eggs
1/4 cup (2 oz.) silken tofu
1/2 cup plain yogurt

2 tbs. goat cheese
1 tbs. flour
1/2 cup cubed firm tofu
1/4 tsp. dried tarragon
salt and pepper to taste
unbaked 9-inch piecrust

Heat oven to 350°. In a skillet over medium heat, cook bacon until crisp. Add onion and caraway seeds and cook until onion is transparent. In a bowl, combine eggs, silken tofu, yogurt and goat cheese. Fold in flour, onions, bacon, cubed tofu, tarragon, salt and pepper. Pour into piecrust. Bake for 45 to 50 minutes, until quiche is firm.

HAM STRATA

You can assemble this dish the night before, refrigerate it, and bake it the next morning, if you wish.

4 whole-wheat bread slices, crusts removed, cubed
1 cup diced cooked extra-lean ham
1 cup (8 oz.) silken tofu, drained
3 eggs
1 cup unflavored soymilk
1 tsp. dry mustard
2 tbs. minced green onion

Heat oven to 350°. Spray an 8-inch-square baking pan with nonstick cooking spray. Arrange bread cubes in prepared pan. Sprinkle ham over bread.

In a bowl, beat tofu until smooth. Add eggs and beat until combined. Beat in soymilk, mustard and onion. Pour over ham and bread. Bake for about 40 minutes, or until set. Serve warm.

APPLE PANCAKES

The creamy qualities of toasted full-fat soy flour are similar to that of egg yolk. The lecithin which occurs naturally in soybeans restricts oil from penetrating the dough as it is being fried. 1 tbs. soy flour mixed with 1 tbs. water can replace an egg in this recipe or add 1 egg, if desired.

3 tbs. sugar
1/2 tsp. cinnamon
1/4 tsp. nutmeg
1/8 tsp. salt
1 cup all-purpose flour
1 tbs. soy flour
2 tsp. baking powder

1 egg, optional
3/4 cup unflavored soymilk
1 tsp. vanilla extract
2 tbs. soy margarine, melted and cooled
1 tart apple, peeled, cored and grated
applesauce and maple syrup for garnish

In a large bowl, mix sugar with cinnamon, nutmeg and salt. Add flour, soy flour, baking powder and egg if desired, stirring to combine well. In a separate bowl, whisk together soymilk, vanilla and margarine. Pour liquid ingredients over dry mixture and blend . Fold in apples. Heat a nonstick griddle or skillet over medium heat. Pour 1/4 cupfuls batter onto griddle and cook for 2 minutes on first side, or until bubbles appear on surface. Flip and cook for 1 minute, or until cooked through. Serve topped with applesauce and maple syrup.

PANCAKES

Top these pancakes with fresh fruit or jam for even more health benefits. For thinner pancakes, add up to ¼ cup extra soymilk.

1 egg
¾ cup unflavored soymilk
2 tbs. soy oil or melted butter
1 cup unbleached flour
1 tbs. sugar
3 tsp. baking powder
½ tsp. salt
warm maple syrup for garnish

In a small bowl, beat egg until frothy. Whisk in soymilk and oil. In a large bowl, combine flour, sugar, baking powder and salt. Add egg mixture to flour mixture, stirring to combine. Heat griddle or skillet over medium heat until water sprinkled on it bubbles. Pour about 3 tbs. of the batter onto griddle for each pancake. Leave room for pancakes to spread out. Turn pancakes over when they rise, form bubbles on top and are brown on the bottom. Serve with warm maple syrup.

CINNAMON ROLLS

Using frozen bread dough means that cinnamon rolls can be a fairly fast and easy treat.

2 loaves frozen bread dough, thawed

Filling
6 tbs. soy margarine, softened, divided
3/4 cup dark brown sugar, packed
1 tsp. cinnamon
1/2 cup chopped pecans

Glaze
2 tbs. soy margarine, softened
1/2 pkg. (12.3 oz. pkg.) silken tofu
4 cups confectioners' sugar
1 tsp. vanilla
1 tbs. instant coffee

Spray a 9 x 13-inch pan with nonstick cooking spray. Roll each loaf into a rectangle (about 9 x 11 inches). Spread 3 tbs. of the margarine on each rectangle of dough. Sprinkle with half of the brown sugar, 1/2 tsp. of the cinnamon and 1/4 cup of the pecans. Roll up each rectangle of dough jelly roll-style, starting with a long side. Cut each roll into 12 slices and place cut sides up in prepared pan. Cover and set aside to rise until double, about 50 minutes. Heat oven to 350°. Bake rolls for 35 to 40 minutes. Cool for 15 minutes. While rolls are cooling, mix margarine, tofu, confectioners' sugar, vanilla and coffee in a blender container. Drizzle glaze over warm rolls.

MAKE-AHEAD FRENCH TOAST

This is a quick way to have real French toast on a busy morning, since most of the work is done the night before.

6 eggs
²/₃ cup unflavored soymilk
²/₃ cup orange juice
¹/₄ tsp. salt
¹/₂ tsp. orange extract or grated orange zest
8 slices French bread, cut ¹/₂ inch thick
2 tbs. soy oil or butter
warm maple syrup for garnish

Whisk eggs in a large bowl. Add milk, orange juice, salt and orange extract. Mix well. Dip bread into egg mixture, turning to coat all surfaces. Place soaked bread in a baking dish in a single layer. Pour any remaining egg mixture over bread. Cover and refrigerate overnight. In the morning, heat oil in a skillet over medium heat. Add French toast and brown well on both sides. Serve with warm maple syrup.

BLUEBERRY COFFEE CAKE

Coffee cake is always a welcome treat for breakfast or brunch, and this one is as healthy as it is delicious.

3/4 cup (6 oz.) silken tofu, drained
3/4 cup sugar
1/4 cup margarine, softened
1/4 cup fat-free vanilla soymilk
2 tsp. vanilla extract
1 1/2 cups all-purpose flour

1/2 cup rolled oats
2 tsp. baking powder
1/4 tsp. salt
1/4 tsp. ground nutmeg
1 1/2 cups fresh or frozen blueberries

Heat oven to 350°. Spray a bundt pan with nonstick cooking spray. Beat tofu in a medium bowl until smooth. Add sugar and margarine and beat until combined. Beat in soymilk and vanilla. Combine flour, oats, baking powder, salt and nutmeg in a medium bowl. Add flour mixture to tofu mixture and beat until combined. Stir in blueberries. Spoon mixture into a prepared pan. Bake for about 35 minutes, or until top springs back when lightly pressed. Cool in pan for 10 minutes. Serve warm.

OATMEAL

Breakfast literally means "breaking the fast." To set your metabolic rate at a nice level for the day, a high-protein breakfast is important. Here is an easy way to energize your morning cereal by adding protein-rich tofu!

1 cup milk or unflavored soymilk
½ cup (4 oz.) silken tofu
½ cup water
½ cup quick oats
1 tbs. maple syrup
2 tbs. raisins, optional
1 tsp. cinnamon, optional

In a small saucepan, whisk together milk, tofu and water and bring to a boil. Stir in oats. Reduce heat and simmer for about 3 minutes. If mixture is too thick add a little more milk. Remove from heat and stir in maple syrup. Stir in raisins and cinnamon, if using.

ENTRÉES

24 Three-Bean Chili
25 Sloppy Joes
26 Tofu Mexican Fiesta
27 Pan-Fried Tofu with Mango Chutney
28 Tofu Kabobs with Shrimp and Scallops
29 Grilled Mushrooms, Tofu and Peppers
30 Grilled Flounder with Curry Sauce
31 Chicken Kabobs
32 Tofu Cutlets
33 Tofu Lasagna
34 Soybean Burgers
35 Two-Soybean Cakes
36 Tuna or Salmon Sandwiches
37 Crab Quesadillas with Avocado Sauce
38 Chicken Tofu Stir-Fry
39 Tofu Grilled Cheese Sandwich

40 Apricot Chicken with Snow Peas
41 Steamed Shrimp with Honey Garlic
      Peanut Sauce
42 Soybeans in Tortillas
43 Italian Tofu Meatballs
44 Cornish Pasties
45 Tempeh Stew
46 Tempeh-Lemon Broil
47 Simple Barbecued Tempeh with
      Onions
48 Marinated Tempeh Kabobs
49 Tempeh Chili
50 TSP Tacos
51 Stuffed Peppers
52 5-Minute Sweet and Sour Tofu Stir-Fry
53 Tofu with Miso Barbecue Sauce

THREE-BEAN CHILI

Adjust the chili powder to your favorite heat level—from mild to five-alarm.

2 tsp. soy oil
1½ cups chopped onion
1 can (15 oz.) white soybeans
1 can (15 oz.) black soybeans, or black
   beans
1 can (15 oz.) red beans
2 cans (14.5 oz. each) diced tomatoes

1 can (15 oz.) tomato sauce
½ cup brown sugar
½ tsp. salt
½ tsp. pepper
2 tsp. ground cumin
2 tbs. minced garlic
1 tsp. chili powder

Heat oil in a large pot over medium-high heat. Add onions and sauté until soft. Rinse and drain white and black soybeans and red beans and add to onion. Stir in tomatoes, tomato sauce, brown sugar, salt, pepper, cumin, garlic and chili powder. Bring to a boil, reduce heat to low and simmer for 30 to 45 minutes.

SLOPPY JOES

Many stores carry only firm or silken tofu. This will not be a problem for your recipes. Simply use silken for dishes that are creamy (including soups and sauces) and firm for most other recipes.

2 tbs. olive oil
1 medium onion, chopped
1 green bell pepper, chopped
3 cloves garlic, minced
2 tbs. soy sauce

1 pkg. (14 oz. pkg.) firm tofu, crumbled
2 cups tomato or pasta sauce
1 tbs. chili powder
$\frac{1}{2}$ tsp. ground cumin
4–6 burger buns

Add olive oil to a skillet over medium-high heat. Add onion, bell pepper and garlic and sauté until tender. Add soy sauce and tofu. Continue cooking until tofu browns. Stir in tomato sauce, chili and cumin. Cook 5 minutes until thickened slightly. Serve hot over toasted burger buns.

TOFU MEXICAN FIESTA

Servings: 4

If you don't have an ovenproof skillet, transfer the mixture to a casserole before placing it in the oven.

1 large onion, finely chopped
1 large bell pepper, finely chopped
1 tbs. olive oil
16 oz. tofu, well mashed
1 can (8 oz.) tomato sauce
4 eggs, lightly beaten

1½ tsp. ground cumin
2 tsp. chili powder
1 tsp. salt
½ tsp. garlic powder
1 cup grated low-fat cheddar cheese

Heat oven to 375°. In a large ovenproof skillet, sauté onion and pepper in oil over medium heat. Remove from heat. Stir in tofu, tomato sauce, eggs, cumin, chili powder, salt, garlic powder and cheese. Mix well. Place in oven and bake for 45 minutes, until bubbly.

PAN-FRIED TOFU WITH MANGO CHUTNEY

Chutney is sweet, sour and a little bit hot all at the same time—a zesty accompaniment to mild tofu. Use fresh peaches if you can't get mangoes.

1/4 cup vinegar
1/4 cup brown sugar, packed
2 tsp. ground ginger
1 cup diced mango
1 cinnamon stick, or 1/4 tsp. ground
    cinnamon
1/4–1/2 tsp. cayenne pepper

2 tsp. lime juice
1 tbs. olive oil
1 pkg. (14 oz. pkg.) firm tofu, drained, cut
    lengthwise into 4 slices
1/2 lb. tender greens, such as spinach or
    mustard greens

In a small saucepan, combine vinegar, brown sugar and ginger. Cook over medium heat, stirring frequently, for 3 minutes. Add mango, cinnamon, cayenne and lime juice. Bring to a boil. Reduce heat and simmer for 3 minutes more. Remove cinnamon stick from chutney, if using, and set chutney aside.

Heat oil in a large skillet over medium heat. Gently brown tofu slices. Place tofu on greens and top with chutney.

TOFU KABOBS WITH SHRIMP AND SCALLOPS

Serve these seafood kabobs over rice or pasta and steamed vegetables.

juice of 2 lemons
2 tbs. olive oil
2–3 large cloves garlic, minced
$\frac{1}{2}$ tsp. dried oregano
1 tbs. chopped fresh dill
1 tbs. chopped fresh parsley

12 large shrimp, peeled
12 large sea scallops
12 cubes firm tofu, cut into 1-inch cubes
salt and pepper to taste

Soak wooden skewers in water for 15 minutes. In a small bowl, combine lemon juice, oil, garlic, oregano, dill and parsley. Thread 3 shrimp, 3 scallops and 3 tofu cubes on each skewer, alternating ingredients. Place skewers in a large baking dish. Spoon half of the marinade over. Turn skewers and cover with remaining marinade. Cover and refrigerate for 5 to 6 hours.

Before grilling, sprinkle with salt and pepper. Grill skewers for about 5 minutes on each side, or until shrimp turn pink.

GRILLED MUSHROOMS, TOFU AND PEPPERS

Servings: 4

Serve over pasta or couscous. If you like, substitute any other vegetables such as zucchini or onions for the peppers.

1 green bell pepper, quartered
1 orange or yellow bell pepper, quartered
1 red bell pepper, quartered
8 medium white mushrooms, quartered
1 pkg. (14 oz. pkg.) firm tofu, cut into $1/4$-inch slices
6 tbs. bottled Italian salad dressing

Brush all sides of mushrooms, peppers and tofu with salad dressing. Set in a bowl with remaining dressing and marinate for 3 to 6 hours. Drain marinade from vegetables and reserve it. Grill the vegetables and tofu for about 5 minutes on each side, or until well browned. Brush with reserved marinade while cooking.

GRILLED FLOUNDER WITH CURRY SAUCE

This rich sauce gets its creamy consistency from low-fat yogurt and tofu. It's an elegant accompaniment to the delicate flounder.

2 tbs. soy oil
3 tbs. plus 1 tsp. lime juice, divided
2 lbs. flounder or other white fish
4 oz. firm tofu

½ cup low-fat yogurt
2 tbs. orange marmalade
1 tsp. mild curry powder
lime zest for garnish

In a small bowl, whisk together oil and 2 tbs. of the lime juice until well blended. Divide flounder into 6 pieces. Brush both sides with lime-oil marinade. Set aside.

In a blender container or food processor workbowl, combine tofu and yogurt, and blend until smooth. Add marmalade, remaining 4 tsp. lime juice and curry powder. Blend until well combined; set curry sauce aside.

Place fish on an oiled grill and grill for 2 to 3 minutes. Turn fish over and grill for 2 to 3 minutes longer, or until fish flakes easily with a fork. Top with curry sauce. Garnish with lime zest.

CHICKEN KABOBS

If your recipe calls for silken or "lite" tofu, and you can only find firm, simply add a little extra liquid to the recipe. The marinade/sauce in this recipe is great with pork. too.

1 cup (8 oz.) silken tofu	$1/4$ tsp. cinnamon
3 cloves garlic	$1/4$ tsp. ground cloves
1 small onion, quartered	$1/4$ tsp. ground nutmeg
1 tbs. minced fresh ginger	$1/4$ tsp. cayenne pepper
1 tbs. lemon juice	$1 1/2$ lbs. boneless skinless chicken breasts
1 tsp. ground cumin	2 onions, cut in wedges
1 tsp. salt	1 pint cherry tomatoes
$1/2$ tsp. ground turmeric	

Blend tofu, garlic, quartered onion, ginger, lemon juice, cumin, salt, turmeric, cinnamon, cloves, nutmeg and cayenne in a food processor workbowl or blender container. Cut chicken into 1-inch cubes and coat with half the marinade, reserving second half to use as a sauce. Marinate chicken in the refrigerator for 30 minutes. Heat broiler or grill. Thread chicken, onion wedges and tomatoes on skewers, discarding marinade. Grill or broil kabobs for 8 to 10 minutes, or until chicken is cooked through. Serve with reserved sauce.

TOFU CUTLETS

I first tasted tofu cutlets at a restaurant in Atlantic City. They were listed as "fresh cutlets" on the menu. The waiter, apparently unaware of their true ingredients, said they were most likely made from white fish or possibly veal. Having tasted these delicious morsels I asked if the chef would give me the recipe. Note that if you freeze tofu, it is less likely to fall apart when cooked.

2 tbs. grated fresh ginger
1/4 cup soy sauce
1 1/2 cups water
4 two-ounce slices frozen firm tofu,
   3/8-inch thick

1/2 cup flour
1 egg, lightly beaten
1/2 cup breadcrumbs
oil for deep frying
1 lemon, cut into 4 wedges

Combine ginger, soy sauce and water in a large saucepan and bring to a boil. Reduce heat to low. Add tofu and simmer for 15 to 20 minutes. Lift out tofu. Allow to cool slightly, then press each piece lightly to expel excess liquid. Dust each slice well with flour, dip in egg and coat with breadcrumbs. Heat 1 to 2 inches of oil in a wok to 375°. Add cutlets and fry until golden brown. Serve with lemon wedges.

TOFU LASAGNA

Tofu takes the place of ricotta in this delicious vegetarian lasagna.

8 lasagna noodles (about ½ lb.)
½ cup (4 oz.) mashed silken tofu
½ cup grated Parmesan cheese
1 egg
2 cloves garlic finely chopped, divided
⅛ tsp. ground nutmeg

1 bag (16 oz.) chopped frozen spinach, thawed, squeezed dry
2½ cups chunky spaghetti sauce
1 cup coarsely chopped fresh parsley
1 cup shredded skim milk mozzarella cheese

Heat oven to 350°. Cook noodles in boiling water until tender. While noodles are cooking, beat tofu, ¼ cup of the Parmesan, egg, and 1 clove of the garlic in a small bowl until smooth.

In another bowl, mix nutmeg with spinach and remaining clove garlic. Spread ¾ cup of the spaghetti sauce on the bottom of a 9 x 13-inch pan and top with 2 noodles. Sprinkle parsley and mozzarella over noodles. cover with 2 noodles and spread spinach mixture over noodles. Cover with 2 more noodles and spread tofu mixture evenly over noodles. Top with remaining 2 noodles. Cover with remaining sauce and sprinkle with remaining ¼ cup Parmesan. Bake for 45 to 50 minutes. Let stand for 8 minutes before serving.

SOYBEAN BURGERS

Serve these yummy veggie burgers hot with or without a roll.

3 tbs. olive oil, divided
¼ cup chopped onion
¼ cup finely chopped green bell pepper
¼ cup finely chopped celery
1 cup cooked or canned soybeans
1 cup cooked brown rice
¼ cup flour
1 egg, beaten
salt and pepper to taste
sesame seeds for coating

Heat 1 tbs. of the oil in a skillet over medium heat. Add onion, green pepper and celery. Sauté until soft. Pour into a large bowl and add soybeans, rice and flour. Stir in egg, salt and pepper. Shape into 4 patties and coat both sides with sesame seeds. Heat remaining 2 tbs. oil in a skillet over medium heat and sauté patties until firm and golden.

TWO-SOYBEAN CAKES

Servings: 4–6

These spicy veggie burgers are delicious with simple lettuce and tomato garnishes.

1 cup (8 oz.) silken tofu
1/2 tsp. lemon juice
1/2 tsp. plus 1 pinch salt
3/4 cup canned black soybeans, drained
3/4 cup canned green soybeans, drained
1–2 tbs. vegetable broth
1/3 cup onion, minced
1 tbs. garlic, minced
1 jalapeño chile, minced

1 tsp. soy oil
3/4 tsp. chili powder
1 tsp. ground cumin
3/4 tsp. ground cardamom
1 1/2 tsp. fresh cilantro, chopped
2 tsp. lime juice
1 egg white, lightly beaten
1/2 cup cornmeal for dusting
2–4 tbs. butter

In a food processor workbowl, combine tofu, lemon juice and 1 pinch of the salt until well blended. Refrigerate. In a food processor workbowl, puree 2/3 of the black and 2/3 of the green beans with broth. Add puree to a bowl with whole beans. In a skillet, sauté onion, garlic and jalapeño in oil over medium heat. Add herbs and spices and sauté until aromatic. Add onion mixture to beans and stir well. Add lime juice and egg white and mix well. Form into patties. Dust patties with cornmeal and sauté in butter until crisp. Serve with tofu sauce.

ENTRÉES   35

TUNA OR SALMON SANDWICHES

Servings: 3

Instead of sandwiches, you might like to try serving wraps: use 8-inch flour tortillas instead of bread, and fold over the filling.

1 can (7½ oz.) tuna or salmon, drained
½ cup medium tofu
2–3 tbs. mayonnaise, or to taste
pepper to taste
1 green onion, thinly sliced
6 slices bread
bean sprouts or spinach leaves for garnish

Mash tuna, tofu and mayonnaise together in a small bowl. Fold in pepper and onion. Spread mixture on 3 bread slices. Top with sprouts or spinach leaves and remaining bread slices.

CRAB QUESADILLAS WITH AVOCADO SAUCE

Servings: 4

Remove seeds of the jalapeño if you want to reduce the heat. And it's a good idea to wear rubber gloves when chopping chiles to keep the oils from irritating your skin.

1 small avocado
½ cup (4 oz.) silken tofu, drained
2 tbs. lemon juice
1 jalapeño chile, minced
4 eight-inch flour tortillas

4 oz. flaked crabmeat
4 oz. Monterey jack-style soy cheese, finely chopped
2 tbs. chopped fresh cilantro, optional

Peel and chop avocado. Process avocado and tofu in a food processor workbowl until smooth. Add lemon juice and process to combine. Place in a small bowl and stir in jalapeño. Cover and refrigerate. Heat griddle over medium heat. Place 2 of the tortillas on hot griddle. Divide crabmeat and cheese between tortillas. Sprinkle with cilantro, if using. Top with remaining tortillas. Cook, turning once, until tortillas are browned and cheese is melted, about 3 minutes on each side. Cut quesadillas into wedges. Serve with reserved avocado sauce.

CHICKEN TOFU STIR-FRY

Serve over rice in the Chinese manner.

$1/2$ tsp. minced fresh ginger
1 tbs. soy sauce
3 tbs. soy oil, divided
2 tbs. water
1 tbs. cornstarch
2 lbs. boneless, skinless chicken breast, cubed
7–8 oz. firm tofu, cubed
1 large bunch broccoli, cut into florets, about 4 cups
1 large red bell pepper, cut into thin strips, about $1 1/2$ cups
1 pkg. (10 oz.) frozen green soybeans, thawed

In a bowl, combine ginger, soy sauce, 2 tbs. of the oil, water and cornstarch. Add chicken and tofu and marinate for $1/2$ hour. Heat remaining 1 tbs. oil in a wok or skillet over high heat. Add tofu and chicken with marinade and stir-fry until browned. Add broccoli, pepper and soybeans. Cover with a lid and cook for 6 to 8 minutes, until vegetables are crisp-tender.

TOFU GRILLED CHEESE SANDWICH

Servings: 4

A classic with more than one twist, these open-faced sandwiches gain a nutritious punch with the addition of tofu.

4 slices whole-grain bread
4 tsp. mustard
¼ cup tofu mayonnaise
4 thin slices tomato
1 pkg. (14 oz. pkg.) firm tofu, cut into 8
   thin slices
4 slices American or cheddar cheese

Heat broiler. Spread each slice of bread with mustard and mayonnaise. Top each sandwich with 1 slice tomato and 2 slices tofu. Add cheese. Broil until cheese melts.

APRICOT CHICKEN WITH SNOW PEAS

The sweetness of the apricots harmonizes beautifully with the crunchy snow peas, and the mustard adds a zing. Serve over rice.

2 tbs. olive oil, divided
1 boneless, skinless chicken breast, cut into thin strips
2–3 cloves garlic, minced
salt and pepper to taste
1 cup cubed firm tofu
12 whole almonds

1/2 cup sliced dried apricots
1/2–3/4 cup water
1/2 cup apricot preserves
1 tbs. Dijon mustard
soy sauce to taste
1/2 lb. snow peas
1 tbs. toasted sesame seeds

Heat 1 tbs. of the oil in a wok or skillet over high heat. Add chicken, garlic, salt and pepper and stir-fry for 5 minutes. Remove chicken with a slotted spoon and set aside. Add the remaining 1 tbs. oil to the wok, add tofu and stir-fry for 2 minutes. Return chicken to the wok. Add almonds, apricots, water, preserves, mustard and soy sauce. Stir and bring to a boil. Add snow peas and cook for about 5 minutes, or until snow peas are crisp-tender. Sprinkle with sesame seeds.

STEAMED SHRIMP
WITH HONEY GARLIC PEANUT SAUCE

Tofu adds a creaminess to the Thai peanut sauce. This dish can be served as an appetizer or as an entrée.

¼ cup (2 oz.) silken tofu
juice of 1 orange
juice of ½ lemon
¼ cup smooth peanut butter
2 tbs. honey
2 cloves garlic, minced

¼ cup chopped fresh basil
1 tsp. minced fresh ginger
1–2 tbs. soy sauce
salt and pepper to taste
1 lb. steamed shrimp, peeled

In a small saucepan, blend well tofu, orange juice, lemon juice, peanut butter, honey, garlic, basil, ginger, soy sauce, salt and pepper. Simmer, covered, over low heat for about 5 minutes. Serve warm as a dip for shrimp.

SOYBEANS IN TORTILLAS

If you are using canned soybeans, the "liquid" in with the beans may actually be a gelatinous material. Once heated it liquefies and can easily be measured.

2 tbs. olive oil
3 onions, minced
1 cup canned soybeans with liquid
3 tbs. miso
1 dash Tabasco Sauce
12 tortillas, warmed and buttered
1½ cups grated cheddar cheese
1 tomato, chopped
1 cup shredded lettuce

Add oil to a large skillet over medium heat and sauté onions until transparent. Place onions in a large bowl and stir in soybeans plus ¼ cup of their liquid, miso and Tabasco. Spoon mixture into tortillas and top with cheese and tomato. Roll up each tortilla and serve immediately.

ITALIAN TOFU MEATBALLS

This is a recipe created and served at Tokyo's Seventh Day Adventist hospital. Serve the meatballs over pasta.

1 pkg. (14 oz. pkg.) firm tofu
1/4 cup chopped walnuts
1/2 onion, minced
1/4 cup breadcrumbs
1 egg, lightly beaten
3 tbs. minced fresh parsley
1 pinch pepper

1/2 tsp. salt
olive oil for frying
1/4 cup tomato juice
1/4 cup ketchup
1 pinch dried oregano
3 tbs. grated Parmesan cheese

Heat oven to 350°. Press tofu between paper towels to remove excess liquid. In a bowl, mash tofu and combine with walnuts, onion, breadcrumbs, egg, parsley, pepper and salt. Mix well and shape into 1½-inch balls. Add 1/4- to 1/2-inch olive oil to a wok or skillet over medium-high heat. Add meatballs and cook until firm and brown. Combine tomato juice, ketchup and oregano in a bowl. Place meatballs in a baking dish, cover with sauce and top with Parmesan. Bake for 20 minutes. Serve with extra grated cheese.

CORNISH PASTIES

Cornish pasties were a classic lunch meal for Welsh miners, since they were filling, portable, and of course delicious. This version adds the health benefits of soy. Burger mix is available from health food stores, or you can order it over the internet.

purchased soy or tofu burger mix, enough for 4 burgers
1 medium onion
2 medium potatoes
1 cup sliced frozen carrots, thawed
½ tsp. dried basil
1 tsp. dried parsley
2 unbaked piecrusts

Heat oven to 375°. In a large bowl, prepare vegetarian mix according to directions on package (but do not cook it). Chop and sauté onion in olive oil. Dice and boil potatoes in water. Add cooked potatoes and onions, carrots, basil and parsley to vegetarian mix. Roll out piecrusts slightly to flatten. Cut pastry dough into 3-inch circles. Place a heaping spoonful of the filling in each circle. Fold pastry over filling. Seal edges by pressing together with fingers. Place on a cookie sheet and bake for 45 minutes, until browned.

TEMPEH STEW

Serve this over brown rice. Other vegetables such as potatoes, greens and broccoli can be added to this stew.

1 pkg. (16 oz.) tempeh
2 tbs. olive oil
1 onion, chopped
2 cloves minced garlic
1 green bell pepper, chopped
1 can (14 oz.) stewed tomatoes

¼ tsp. dried oregano
¼ tsp. dried basil
¼ cup chopped fresh parsley
salt and pepper to taste
2 tbs. soy sauce

Add oil to a large skillet over medium heat. Crumble tempeh into skillet with onion, garlic and bell pepper and sauté for 5 to 8 minutes. Add stewed tomatoes, oregano, basil, parsley, salt, pepper and soy sauce. Reduce heat to low and simmer for about 1 hour.

TEMPEH-LEMON BROIL

Tempeh is a nutritious substitute for chicken or steak. This marinade gives the tempeh a robust flavor.

16 oz. tempeh
1 large onion, sliced
juice of 3 lemons
¼ cup olive oil
3 tbs. soy sauce
2 cloves garlic, minced

Cut tempeh into 16 chunks. Place in a bowl with sliced onions. In a small bowl, mix together lemon juice, olive oil, soy sauce and garlic. Pour over tempeh and onions. Marinate for at least 3 hours in the refrigerator.

Heat oven to 400°. Drain tempeh and onions, reserving marinade. Spread on a cookie sheet. Bake for 30 minutes, basting occasionally with reserved marinade.

SIMPLE BARBECUED TEMPEH WITH ONIONS

The tempeh and onions can also be marinated in the barbecue sauce for one hour and then cooked on the grill.

8 oz. tempeh
2 medium onions
2 cups preferred barbecue sauce

Heat oven to 350°. Cut tempeh into 20 cubes. Slice onion thinly. Place tempeh, onion slices and barbecue sauce in a casserole dish. Cover and bake for 30 minutes.

MARINATED TEMPEH KABOBS

Tender tempeh makes a nice contrast with crisp vegetables in these kabobs.

2 tbs. lemon juice
2 tbs. olive oil
1/4 cup soy sauce
1/4 cup tarragon vinegar
1 tbs. dried basil
1 tbs. dried thyme
1 tbs. dried rosemary

3 cloves garlic, crushed
pepper to taste
8 oz. tempeh, cut into 8 cubes
12 medium mushrooms
1 red bell pepper, cut into 8 pieces
1 medium onion, quartered
1 small zucchini, cut into 8 pieces

Combine lemon juice, oil, soy sauce, vinegar, basil, thyme, rosemary, garlic and pepper in a jar and shake well to mix. Steam tempeh cubes over boiling water for 10 minutes; drain well. Toss tempeh, mushrooms, pepper, onion and zucchini with marinade and refrigerate for at least 1 hour. Arrange tempeh and vegetables on skewers and grill for 10 to 15 minutes, turning frequently and brushing with marinade.

TEMPEH CHILI

Servings: 2

Tempeh has twice as much protein as hamburger meat. It is also the best food source of vitamin B12 for a vegetarian. Serve this chili over rice.

8 oz. tempeh
2 tbs. soy oil
1 large onion, diced
2½ cups tomato sauce
3 tbs. chili powder
1 tbs. soy sauce
1 tbs. dry mustard
2 tsp. garlic powder
1 tsp. ground cumin

Cut tempeh into small cubes. Add oil to a large saucepan over medium heat. Crumble tempeh into saucepan and sauté for about 10 minutes, until just browned. Add onion, tomato sauce, chili powder, soy sauce, mustard, garlic powder and cumin and simmer for 20 minutes.

TSP TACOS

TSP (textured soy protein) is made from highly refined granules of soy that are 90% protein. TSP has been used as an ingredient in many processed foods since 1950, especially vegetarian burgers. TSP is available in slices and chunks, but is usually found in granular form. With the addition of hot water it forms a texture similar to ground beef, for which it is often used as a substitute.

1¼ cups granular TSP (textured soy protein)
1 cup boiling water
1½ cups tomato sauce
1½ tsp. chili powder
1½ tsp. garlic powder

1 tsp. sugar
8 corn tortillas
shredded lettuce for garnish
chopped tomatoes for garnish
salsa for garnish

Place TSP in a large bowl. Pour boiling water over TSP, stir and set aside. In a saucepan over medium-low heat, combine tomato sauce, chili powder, garlic powder and sugar and simmer for 10 minutes. Add TSP and cook for another 10 minutes. Warm tortillas on a cookie sheet in the oven. Remove and fill with TSP mixture. Garnish with lettuce, tomatoes and salsa.

STUFFED PEPPERS

These are stuffed peppers like Mom used to make—and you won't miss the meat. Use any color of bell pepper you wish: each color has a slightly different taste.

1 cup TSP (textured soy protein)
⅞ cup boiling water
1 medium onion, chopped
2 cloves garlic, minced
1 tsp. soy oil

1 cup cooked rice
1 cup tomato sauce
¼ cup chopped walnuts
4 large bell peppers
2 cups vegetable broth

Heat oven to 350°. In a bowl, soak TSP in boiling water. In a skillet over medium heat, sauté onions and garlic in soy oil until tender. Add to TSP in bowl, along with rice, tomato sauce and walnuts. Cut off tops of peppers and scoop out seeds and ribs. Stuff each pepper with filling.

Stand peppers up in a baking pan and pour vegetable broth around base of peppers. Cover pan and bake for 30 minutes.

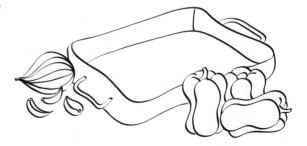

5-MINUTE SWEET AND SOUR TOFU STIR-FRY

If you like Chinese food, you must try this quick and easy dish, which is both light and nutritious. Serve this stir-fry over rice—or for something different, try serving over Chinese noodles.

2 tbs. soy oil
1 medium onion, coarsely chopped
1 red bell pepper, thinly sliced
1/2 green bell pepper, thinly sliced
1 pkg. (14 oz. pkg.) firm tofu, cut into bite-size pieces
salt and pepper to taste
1 jar (16 oz.) sweet and sour sauce

Over high heat, in a wok or deep nonstick skillet, heat oil. Add onion and peppers and stir-fry for 2 minutes. Add tofu and stir-fry for 1 minute. Sprinkle with salt and pepper. Stir in sweet and sour sauce. Reduce heat to medium and cook for a few minutes longer, until heated through.

TOFU WITH MISO BARBECUE SAUCE

After marinating, the tofu can be grilled instead of baked, for additional smoky flavor.

1 pkg. (14 oz. pkg.) firm tofu
1 tbs. miso
1/4 cup water
1 tbs. sesame seeds
3 green onions, chopped

4 cloves garlic, minced
2 tbs. sesame oil
2 tbs. maple syrup
2 tbs. sherry
1/8 tsp. pepper

Cut tofu into chunks and place in a large bowl. In a small bowl, mix together miso and water, stirring until smooth. Add sesame seeds, onions, garlic, sesame oil, maple syrup, sherry and pepper to miso. Mix well. Pour sauce over tofu and set aside to marinate for 2 to 3 hours.

Heat oven to 350°. Drain tofu and place in a baking dish. Bake for 30 minutes, basting frequently with sauce.

SIDE DISHES

SCALLOPED POTATOES

Leftover Scalloped Potatoes are great for making soup. Simply add milk to desired consistency and heat. Soymilk can be used instead of regular milk in any recipe that calls for milk.

10 medium red-skinned potatoes
2 sweet onions (such as Vidalia)
salt and pepper to taste

about ¾ cup flour, divided
1½–2 cups unflavored soymilk

Heat oven to 425°. Oil the bottom of a 2-quart casserole dish. Thinly slice potatoes and onions. Place a layer of potatoes in prepared dish. Top layer generously with sliced onions. Sprinkle with salt, pepper and 2 tbs. of the flour. Repeat layers, using all remaining potatoes and onions. Pour in enough milk to completely cover all layers.

Place casserole dish on a cookie sheet to catch any spills and bake for 10 minutes. Reduce heat to 375° and bake until potatoes are tender, about 45 minutes.

STUFFED BAKED POTATOES

What was once just a carbohydrate is now also a rich protein source with this recipe. These potatoes can be stuffed, then refrigerated or frozen before baking.

6 baking potatoes
1/2 pkg (12.3 oz. pkg.) silken tofu
1 tbs. soy oil
1/2 tsp. pepper
3/4 cup shredded soy American cheese
1/4 cup chopped green onions
1/4 cup bacon bits
1/2 cup chopped bell peppers (red, green and/or yellow)

Heat oven to 350°. Scrub potatoes , brush with soy oil and bake for 1 hour, or until tender. Leave oven at 350°. Cut potatoes in half and scoop potato flesh into a bowl, reserving skins. To potato flesh, add tofu and blend well. Add 1/2 cup of the cheese, green onions, bacon bits and 1/4 cup of the peppers. Fill reserved potato skins with this mixture.

Bake for 20 minutes. Top with remaining peppers and cheese. Bake for 5 minutes longer to melt cheese.

GARLIC AND HERB MASHED POTATOES

These mashed potatoes have 6 grams of protein and only 3 grams of fat.

1½ lbs. potatoes, peeled and coarsely chopped
1 tbs. butter or soy butter
2 tbs. chopped fresh parsley
1 tsp. chopped fresh dill
½ tsp. fresh thyme
2 large cloves garlic, minced
¾ cup (6 oz.) silken tofu
1 tsp. salt
pepper to taste

In a large saucepan over high heat, add potatoes with water to cover. Bring to a boil. Cover, reduce heat and simmer potatoes until tender. Drain potatoes well, mash and set aside.

Melt butter in a small saucepan. Add parsley, dill, thyme and garlic. Cook on medium for 1 minute. Add to potatoes along with tofu, salt and pepper and combine well.

MACARONI AND CHEESE

Your children will never know they're getting a healthy boost from their favorite dish.

2 cups elbow macaroni
2 cups *Béchamel Sauce,* page 93
1/4 cup milk
1 1/4 cups grated cheddar cheese, divided
1/4 tsp. dried oregano
1/2 tsp. tarragon

pepper to taste
1/4 cup cubed tofu
1 tbs. breadcrumbs
1 tbs. rolled oats
1 tsp. butter, melted

Cook macaroni according to directions. Drain and set aside. Heat oven to 375°. Place *Béchamel Sauce* in a large bowl. Add milk and 1 cup of the cheese. Stir in tarragon and pepper. Fold in cubed tofu and macaroni. Transfer to a 2-quart casserole dish. In a small bowl, combine breadcrumbs and oats. Sprinkle over top of casserole and drizzle with butter. Top with remaining 1/4 cup grated cheese. Bake for 20 to 30 minutes, or until browned.

CREAMED SPINACH

For people who dislike spinach, cooks often dress it up with lots of fattening cream—but it's not necessary when you try the following creamy, yet low-fat recipe. For a very low-fat version of this deceptively rich-tasting dish, omit the cheese from the Béchamel Sauce. Also, try substituting Swiss chard, broccoli or leeks for the spinach. Or add broth, herbs, salt and pepper—and you have cream of spinach soup.

2 cups *Béchamel Sauce,* page 93
2 pkg. (10 oz. pkg.) frozen spinach, thawed
salt and pepper to taste

Heat *Béchamel Sauce* in a saucepan over low heat. Squeeze spinach dry and chop. Fold spinach into *Béchamel Sauce.* Cook over low heat, stirring, until sauce begins to bubble. Adjust seasonings to taste.

SOYBEAN, CORN AND TOMATO CASSEROLE

Servings: 4

This is a great side dish or vegetarian main course.

1 cup cooked soybeans
1 cup cooked corn
1 cup diced tomatoes
$1/4$ tsp. paprika
$1/4$ tsp. salt
$1/2$ tsp. sugar
1 tsp. minced onion
$1/2$ cup grated cheddar cheese
$1/4$ cup chopped peanuts

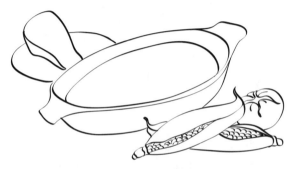

Heat oven to 350°. Lightly oil a 2-quart casserole dish. In a large bowl, combine soybeans, corn, tomatoes, paprika, salt, sugar and onion. Pour into prepared casserole. Top with cheese and peanuts. Bake for 45 minutes.

BROCCOLI RABE WITH TEMPEH

Broccoli rabe is a slightly bitter green vegetable with broccoli-like buds at the end of its slim edible stalk. Substitute regular broccoli florets if you can't find broccoli rabe.

16 oz. tempeh, cubed
1 tbs. olive oil
1/2 cup sliced red onion
4 cloves garlic, minced
4 cups broccoli rabe, tough stems removed
1 red bell pepper, diced
1 1/4 cups unflavored soymilk
2 tbs. arrowroot or cornstarch
1/2 tsp. pepper
salt to taste

In a large skillet over medium heat, sauté tempeh in oil for 4 minutes. Add onion and garlic and sauté for 1 minute longer. Stir in broccoli rabe and bell pepper and cook until tender, 6 to 8 minutes. Combine in a small bowl soymilk, arrowroot, salt and pepper. Add to tempeh mixture and cook, stirring, until thick and bubbly.

BEANS, LENTILS AND TOFU IN TOMATO SAUCE

You can whip up this flavorful dish in a flash if you keep a few cans of lentils and tomato sauce handy in your kitchen cupboard. Serve this over rice, pasta or couscous.

1 can (19 oz.) lentils, rinsed and drained
1 can (19 oz.) white beans, rinsed and
    drained
1 can (19 oz.) tomato sauce
2 medium tomatoes, chopped
1 medium onion, chopped
2 cloves garlic, minced

2 tbs. chopped fresh herbs (basil, thyme
    and/or parsley)
1/4 tsp. dried oregano
soy sauce to taste
hot pepper sauce to taste
1 cup cubed medium or firm tofu

In a large saucepan, combine all ingredients. Cover and simmer over low heat for about 30 minutes, stirring occasionally. If tomatoes are very juicy, remove lid and continue to simmer until liquid has reduced and sauce is thickened.

BAKED BEANS

The perfect picnic dish gets a healthful boost from soy.

8 slices bacon, chopped
1 cup canned navy beans, with liquid
2 cups cooked or canned soybeans, with liquid
1 cup canned kidney beans, with liquid
1/2 cup chopped onion
1/2 cup light molasses
1 tsp. dry mustard
1/2 cup brown sugar, packed
1/2 tsp. chopped garlic
2 tbs. vinegar
1/2 tsp. salt

Heat oven to 325°. In a skillet, sauté bacon over medium-high heat until crisp. In a large bowl, combine bacon, navy, soy and kidney beans with their liquids. Add onion, molasses, mustard, brown sugar, garlic, vinegar and salt. Pour into a casserole and bake, uncovered, for 1 hour, stirring occasionally.

BOSTON BAKED BEANS WITH MEATLESS FRANKS

All-American beans and franks are now vegetarian.

3 cups cooked or canned soybeans with liquid
1 medium onion, chopped
2 tbs. molasses
$\frac{1}{2}$ cup ketchup
$\frac{1}{2}$ tsp. dry mustard
1 tsp. Worcestershire sauce
4 soy hot dogs, sliced
salt and pepper to taste

Heat oven to 325°. In a large bowl, combine soybeans with $\frac{1}{2}$ cup of their liquid. Add onion, molasses, ketchup, mustard, and Worcestershire. Pour into a deep casserole, cover and bake for 30 minutes. Stir and bake, uncovered, for an additional 15 minutes. Add hot dogs and bake for 15 minutes.

ASPARAGUS AND MUSHROOM BAKE

Servings: 4

This simple-to-prepare dish is sophisticated enough for any dinner party.

1 lb. fresh asparagus
8 oz. white mushrooms, halved
½ cup unflavored soymilk
1 tbs. all-purpose flour
2 tbs. minced onion
salt and pepper to taste
½ cup seasoned breadcrumbs

Heat oven to 350°. Oil a shallow 2-quart casserole dish. Trim tough ends from asparagus. In a saucepan with a steamer basket, steam asparagus for 2 to 3 minutes, until crisp-tender. Spread asparagus in the prepared casserole dish. Lay mushrooms on top. In a saucepan, beat together soymilk, flour and onion until well mixed. Place over medium heat and cook, stirring, until thickened and bubbly. Season with salt and pepper to taste. Pour sauce over vegetables in casserole dish. Sprinkle with breadcrumbs. Bake for about 30 minutes, or until well heated.

VEGETARIAN RICE AND BEANS

Servings: 4

This dish is extremely simple to prepare, and as healthy as can be. If you're feeling adventurous, add a minced jalapeño chile to this dish for some heat.

2 cups cooked brown rice
2 tomatoes, chopped
1/4 cup chopped onion
1 large clove garlic, minced
1/2 cup cooked green soybeans
1/2 cup canned soybeans
1 tbs. fresh dill
salt and pepper to taste

Combine all ingredients in a large bowl. Serve cold as a salad or warm beans first and serve as a side dish.

SALADS

ASPARAGUS SALAD

This asparagus salad is also delicious served warm, covered with heated tofu dressing.

1 lb. fresh asparagus
red lettuce leaves
$^2/_3$ cup *Tofu Salad Dressing,* page 103
4 slices red onion
8 strips red bell pepper

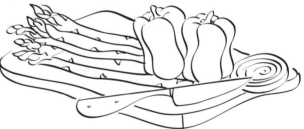

Cut off tough ends of asparagus. In a saucepan with a steamer basket, steam asparagus until tender. Refrigerate until cold.

Arrange asparagus on lettuce leaves on 4 salad plates. Top each serving with *Tofu Salad Dressing* and a slice of red onion. Garnish with red pepper strips.

FALL FRUIT SALAD

Similar to a Waldorf salad, this crunchy dish makes a flavorful and delicious lunch or light supper, accompanied by a good crusty bread.

1/2 cup mayonnaise (soy or regular)
2 tbs. white vinegar
1 tbs. sherry
1 tbs. honey
1 tbs. fresh tarragon, or 1 tsp. dried
1 tbs. Dijon mustard
8 oz. tempeh
4 oz. soy mozzarella cheese, cut into small

cubes
1/2 lb. grapes (mix of green and red), halved
1 small red apple, diced
3/4 cup sliced almonds
1 stalk celery, finely chopped
4 green onions, finely chopped
6 cups lettuce, torn

In a small bowl, whisk together mayonnaise, vinegar, sherry, honey, tarragon and mustard. Set aside. In a saucepan with a steamer basket, steam tempeh until soft, about 20 minutes. Cool and cut into cubes. In a large bowl, combine tempeh, mozzarella, grapes, apples, almonds, celery and green onions. Drizzle dressing over salad and toss lightly. Serve on a bed of torn lettuce leaves.

SPRING SALAD

Steaming the asparagus instead of boiling it retains morevitamins in this nutritious salad.

24 fresh asparagus spears
1 yellow or orange bell pepper, thinly sliced
2 medium tomatoes, sliced
1 small red onion, thinly sliced
½ cup crumbled firm tofu
¼ cup *Tofu Salad Dressing,* page 103

Trim tough ends from asparagus. In a saucepan with a steamer basket, steam asparagus until spears are tender. Remove and drain.

Immediately stack hot asparagus in the center of a large oval platter. Arrange pepper and tomatoes around asparagus. Top with onion and tofu. Spoon *Tofu Salad Dressing* over entire salad. Cool to room temperature. Cover and refrigerate until ready to serve.

TOFU BANANA SALAD

This unusual dish can be served as a side salad or dessert.

6 oz. firm tofu, mashed
3 bananas, thinly sliced
1 tbs. honey
4 large lettuce leaves
¾ cup *Tofu Whipped Cream,* page 144
3 tbs. toasted wheat germ

Combine tofu, bananas and honey in a large bowl. Mix gently. Spoon mixture onto lettuce leaves. Top with *Tofu Whipped Cream* and sprinkle with wheat germ. Serve chilled.

"CHICKEN" SALAD

Textured soy protein takes on the flavors you add to it. This finished salad will taste just like a good homemade chicken salad.

2 cups chicken broth
2 cups TSP (textured soy protein), granulated or in chunks
1/4 cup chopped onion
1/4 cup chopped celery
2 tbs. sweet pickle relish
1/4 tsp. dried dill
salt and pepper to taste
1/2 lb. green or red grapes, halved
1/2 cup low-fat mayonnaise

In a saucepan, bring chicken broth to a boil. Add TSP, reduce heat and cook for about 5 minutes, until TSP is tender and liquid is absorbed. Let stand for 5 minutes. In a large bowl, combine TSP, onion, celery, relish, dill, salt, pepper, grapes and mayonnaise. Refrigerate before serving.

TABBOULEH WITH TOFU

Quinoa, a favorite grain of the ancient Incas, adds a deliciously nutty flavor to a classic Middle Eastern dish. Find it in health food stores or food co-ops, or the health food section of your grocery store.

1 cup uncooked quinoa, rinsed well
1 tbs. curry powder
1 tbs. reduced-sodium soy sauce
1 tsp. minced garlic
4 oz. firm tofu, well drained and cut into small cubes
1 1/2 cups finely chopped fresh flat-leaf parsley

1 medium tomato, seeded and diced
1 medium cucumber, peeled and diced
1 scallion, thinly sliced
3 tbs. fresh lime juice (about 2 limes)
1 tbs. finely chopped fresh mint
1/2 tsp. salt
pepper to taste
6 large red leaf lettuce leaves

In a medium saucepan, combine quinoa, curry powder, soy sauce, garlic and 5 cups water. Bring to a boil over high heat. Reduce heat to low and simmer until quinoa is tender and transparent, about 15 minutes. Drain quinoa, transfer to a large bowl and cool slightly. Add tofu, parsley, tomato, cucumber, scallion, lime juice, mint, salt and pepper. Toss well, fluffing quinoa with fork. Line serving plates with lettuce. Spoon quinoa mixture on top and serve.

APPLE RAISIN SALAD WITH TOFU DRESSING

The peanut butter-tofu dressing in this dressing is also especially tasty with cucumber salad.

¾ cup (6 oz.) silken tofu
3 tbs. smooth peanut butter
1 tbs. lemon juice
1–2 tbs. sugar
2 apples, diced
½ cup raisins
½ cup peanuts or chopped walnuts
1 stalk celery, diced
½ tsp. salt

In a small bowl, combine tofu, peanut butter, lemon juice and sugar, beating until smooth. In a large bowl, combine apples, raisins, nuts, celery and salt. Add dressing and toss to mix.

SOYBEAN SALAD

Soybeans add protein to this crunchy vegetable salad.

1 cup cooked soybeans
1 small apple, diced
$1/3$ cup raisins
1 carrot, grated
$1/3$ cup minced onion
1 cucumber, thinly sliced
1 green bell pepper, thinly sliced
5 tbs. tofu mayonnaise
$1/4$ tsp. salt
1 pinch pepper
6 cups torn lettuce

Combine soybeans, apple, raisins, carrot, onion, cucumber, bell pepper, mayonnaise, salt and pepper. Mix well. Serve on a bed of lettuce.

POTATO SALAD

Serve this potato salad at your next picnic—it will become your new favorite!

2 lbs. potatoes, peeled
3 tbs. rice vinegar
3 stalks celery, chopped
3 small carrots, chopped
1/2 cup chopped onion
2 tbs. chopped fresh parsley
2 tsp. fresh dill
1/2 cup sweet relish
1/2 cup *Tofu Salad Dressing,* page 103

Cook potatoes in a large pot of boiling water for 15 to 20 minutes, until tender. Drain and cool slightly. Chop potatoes and transfer to a bowl. Sprinkle with vinegar. Cool potatoes to room temperature. Stir in celery, carrots, onion, parsley, dill, relish and *Tofu Salad Dressing.* Refrigerate until ready to serve.

TOFU POTATO SALAD

Your family won't notice the difference between this deliciously healthy potato salad and a regular potato salad. This recipe makes enough dressing for two salads, so you can save half the dressing in the refrigerator.

3/4 cup (6 oz.) silken tofu
1 1/2 tbs. lemon juice or vinegar
2 tbs. soy oil
1/2 tsp. salt
1 pinch pepper
1/2 pkg. (14 oz. pkg.) firm tofu, cubed

2 cups cubed cooked potatoes
1 large cucumber, thinly sliced
1/2 cup thinly sliced celery
1/4 cup diced onion
2 tsp. soy sauce

In a blender container, puree silken tofu, lemon juice, soy oil, salt and pepper. Set dressing aside. In a large bowl, combine firm tofu, potatoes, cucumber, celery, onion and soy sauce. Drizzle 6 tbs. of the reserved dressing over salad and toss to coat. Refrigerate salad until ready to serve.

CHICKEN, TOFU AND NOODLE SALAD

Jicama is a starchy vegetable that adds a sweet crunch to this hearty salad. You can buy baked or fried tofu in stores, or make your own by baking a block of tofu in a 350° oven for 20 minutes, or until golden.

1 pkg. (6 oz.) prepared baked or fried tofu, cut crosswise into thin strips

1 boneless, skinless chicken breast, cooked and cut into strips

1 small jicama, cut into thin strips

1 red bell pepper, thinly sliced

1 large carrot, cut into thin strips

1 medium zucchini, cut into thin strips

½ cup *Sesame Dressing*, page 96, divided

6 oz. buckwheat noodles, cooked and drained

¼ cup minced green onions, including tops

¼ cup roasted soy nuts

Combine tofu, chicken, jicama, bell pepper, carrot and zucchini in a medium bowl. Add 2 tbs. of the *Sesame Dressing* and toss to combine. Place noodles in another bowl. Add 2 tbs. of the *Sesame Dressing* and toss to combine. Divide noodles among 4 plates. Top noodles with chicken-vegetable mixture. Sprinkle with green onions and soy nuts. Drizzle with remaining dressing.

EGG SALAD

This egg salad has $1/2$ the cholesterol of an average egg salad. Serve this filling in tortillas for wraps, or between slices of bread for sandwiches.

4 hard-cooked eggs, peeled
1 cup grated firm tofu
1 small onion, finely chopped
$1/4$ cup mayonnaise
1 tsp. Dijon mustard
1 tbs. chopped capers
salt and pepper to taste

Chop eggs and place in a small bowl. Add tofu, onion, mayonnaise, mustard, capers, salt and pepper. Stir gently to combine.

SOUPS

MISO SOUP

A mainstay of Japanese cuisine, miso soup is simple to prepare. Add cubed tofu for extra protein and creamy texture.

1 tsp. soy oil
2 cloves garlic, minced
½ cup thinly sliced onion
1 tsp. grated fresh ginger
½ cup thinly sliced carrots
1 cup thinly sliced mushrooms
2 tbs. miso
4 cups water

Heat oil in a saucepan over medium heat. Add garlic and onions. Sauté until soft. Add ginger, carrots and mushrooms. Cook for about 8 minutes, until vegetables are tender.

Add miso to ¼ cup of the water and mix well. Add miso mixture to vegetables along with remaining water. Simmer soup for 2 minutes.

MINIATURE DUMPLING SOUP

To make this delicious soup from scratch takes about 5 minutes longer than to heat up a can of soup. Of course, it's much better for you than any canned soup! It calls for lovage, a perennial herb that has a strong celery-like flavor. Substitute celery leaves or feel free to use any fresh herb instead.

2 eggs
1/4 cup (2 oz.) silken tofu
1/4 cup unbleached flour
1 pinch salt
4 cups chicken or vegetable broth
1–2 tbs. chopped fresh lovage, fresh celery leaves, or fresh herb of choice
1/2 cup cubed firm tofu
1 tsp. chopped fresh chives for garnish

In a small bowl, blend eggs and silken tofu. Fold in flour and salt. Set batter aside. In a medium saucepan, bring broth and lovage to a boil. Slowly drop small spoonfuls of batter into boiling broth, stirring gently until little dumplings rise to the surface, about 1 minute. Stir in cubed tofu. Heat through and serve garnished with chives.

LEEK AND POTATO SOUP

For a vegetarian version of this soup, use vegetable broth or 2³/₄ cups water for the chicken broth.

2 large leeks
1 tbs. butter
1 cup thinly sliced onion
1 large clove garlic, minced
1 lb. russet potatoes, peeled and cut into
   small cubes
1 bay leaf

2 cans (14.5 oz. each) fat-free, reduced
   sodium chicken broth
1 thyme sprig, or ¼ tsp. dried thyme
½ tsp. salt, or to taste
white pepper to taste
1 cup unflavored soymilk
minced chives, optional, for garnish

Cut root ends and tough green tops from leeks. Split leeks lengthwise and rinse well to remove all sand. Slice leeks thinly. Melt butter in a large saucepan over low heat. Add leeks, onion and garlic. Cover and cook, stirring occasionally, until leeks and onion are very soft, about 10 minutes. Add potatoes, bay leaf, broth, thyme, salt and white pepper. Cover and simmer until potatoes are very tender, 15 to 20 minutes. Discard bay leaf and thyme sprig. Mash potatoes slightly with a potato masher or wooden spoon. Stir in soymilk and heat until hot. Garnish with chives, if desired.

CURRIED PUMPKIN SOUP

This gorgeous soup will impress your guests, but is simple to make.

1 tbs. margarine or butter
1/2 cup chopped onion
1/2 cup chopped celery
1 clove garlic, minced
2 cans (14.5 oz. each) vegetable broth or fat-
   free, reduced-sodium chicken broth

1/2 tsp. salt
white pepper to taste
1 cup (8 oz.) silken tofu
1 cup cooked or canned pureed pumpkin
about 1 cup plain, unsweetened soymilk
2 tsp. curry powder

Melt margarine in a large saucepan over medium heat. Add onion, celery and garlic. Cook, stirring occasionally, for about 5 minutes. Add broth, salt and pepper. Cover and simmer, stirring occasionally, until vegetables are tender, about 20 minutes. With a slotted spoon, transfer vegetables to a food processor workbowl, leaving broth in pan. Add tofu to food processor workbowl and pulse until vegetables are finely chopped and tofu is smooth. Add pumpkin to workbowl and process until combined. Add pumpkin mixture, soymilk and curry powder to broth in saucepan and heat until hot, adding more soymilk if soup is too thick.

CRAB BISQUE

Use fresh crabmeat if possible for optimal flavor, but canned crabmeat will work as well.

1 medium russet potato, peeled and diced
1 large leek, finely chopped
1/2 cup chopped onion
1/2 cup chopped celery
1 small clove garlic, minced
1/2 tsp. salt, or to taste
4 cups water

1/2 cup (4 oz.) silken tofu
8 oz. flaked crabmeat
2 cups unflavored soymilk
2 tsp. minced fresh tarragon, or 1/2 tsp. dried tarragon
1 dash hot pepper sauce, or to taste

Bring potato, leek, onion, celery, garlic, salt and water to a boil in a large saucepan over high heat. Reduce heat to low, cover and cook, stirring occasionally, for 20 minutes, or until vegetables are tender. With a slotted spoon, transfer vegetables to a food processor workbowl, leaving liquid in pan. Add tofu to food processor workbowl and pulse until vegetables are finely chopped and tofu is smooth. Add vegetable mixture, crabmeat, soymilk, tarragon and hot sauce to liquid in saucepan. Heat soup until hot, adding more soymilk if soup is too thick.

CREAMY TOMATO SOUP

Skip the heavy cream usually found in creamy tomato soup—you won't miss it.

2 tsp. soy oil
1 medium onion, sliced
1 large tomato, diced
1/2 tsp. chopped garlic
1 tsp. chopped fresh basil
1/2 tsp. salt
1/2 tsp. pepper
1 cup unflavored soymilk
1 pkg. (12.3 oz. pkg.) silken tofu

Heat oil in a large saucepan over medium heat. Add onion and sauté until transparent. Add tomato and garlic and sauté for 3 minutes. Add basil, salt, pepper and soymilk. Cook for 1 minute. Remove from heat. Add tofu and puree mixture in a food processor workbowl until smooth. Return to the stove and heat.

GREAT VEGETABLE SOUP

This hearty soup is just the thing on a chilly day.

2 tsp. olive oil
1 cup chopped onion
1 cup chopped carrots
1 cup chopped celery
1 large clove garlic, minced
4 cups canned vegetable broth
1¼ cups chopped red potatoes
2 cups chopped tomatoes
1 bay leaf

1 tsp. dried basil
1 tsp. dried thyme
½ tsp. dried oregano
salt and pepper to taste
1 dash hot pepper sauce
1 cup chopped zucchini
1 cup shredded cabbage
1 cup sliced mushrooms
1 can (15 oz.) yellow soybeans

Heat oil in a large nonstick saucepan over low heat. Add onions, carrots, celery and garlic. Cook, stirring occasionally, for 6 minutes. Add broth, potatoes, tomatoes, herbs, salt, pepper and hot pepper sauce. Cover and simmer until potatoes are almost tender, about 14 minutes. Discard bay leaf. Add zucchini, cabbage, mushrooms and soybeans. Simmer for about 10 minutes, until vegetables are tender. Serve piping hot.

BROCCOLI SOUP

This recipe creates a rich, creamy soup containing 14 grams of protein and only 2 grams of fat.

½ lb. russet potatoes, peeled and cubed
1 pkg. (10 oz.) frozen chopped broccoli, thawed
2 cans (14.5 oz. each) fat-free chicken broth
½ cup chopped onion
½ cup chopped celery

1 clove garlic, minced
2 tbs. butter
1 cup (8 oz.) silken tofu
1 cup unflavored soymilk
1 tbs. white miso dissolved in 2 tbs. hot water

In a large saucepan, over medium heat, cook potatoes and broccoli in broth until potatoes are tender. Meanwhile, in a skillet over medium heat, sauté onions, celery and garlic in butter until tender. Pulse onion-celery mixture and tofu in a food processor workbowl until smooth. Add tofu mixture to the saucepan with broccoli and potatoes. Gradually add soymilk and miso and heat. If soup is too thick, thin it by adding more soymilk.

SALMON CHOWDER

I chose salmon for this chowder; however, any fresh fish could be used in this recipe. This dish is an excellent source of Omega-3 fatty acids.

1/2 cup finely chopped onion
1 medium leek, finely chopped
1/2 cup finely chopped carrots
1/2 cup finely chopped celery
2 tbs. finely chopped red bell pepper
1 tbs. olive oil or butter
1 lb. red potatoes, unpeeled, cut into small cubes

3 cups fat-free chicken broth
1 bay leaf
salt and white pepper to taste
6 oz. cooked or canned salmon, drained
1 tbs. chopped fresh tarragon, or 1 tsp. dried tarragon
2 cups unflavored soymilk

In a stockpot over medium heat, sauté onion, leek, carrots, celery and bell pepper in oil until tender, about 4 minutes. Add potatoes, chicken broth, bay leaf, salt and pepper. Reduce heat, cover and simmer until potatoes are tender, about 8 to 10 minutes. Discard bay leaf. Stir in salmon, tarragon and soymilk. Heat and serve piping hot.

SAUCES, SPREADS, DIPS AND SNACKS

SPICY SUN-DRIED TOMATO HUMMUS

Makes about 2½ cups

You would be amazed at the creatures who love tomato hummus: our cat, Fudge, is one. This is delicious with pita wedges, veggies or crackers.

½ cup (4 oz.) silken tofu
2 tbs. lemon juice
1 can (19 oz.) chickpeas, drained
2 tbs. minced, sun-dried tomatoes
4 large cloves garlic, minced
1 tbs. fresh dill
soy sauce to taste

In a food processor workbowl or blender container, puree all ingredients until smooth. Refrigerate for about 4 hours before serving to allow flavors to blend.

SPINACH DIP

Servings: 4

Serve with crackers, pita crisps, toast points or vegetable sticks. Commercially prepared beef base can be found in most grocery stores. It adds flavor to gravies, sauces, soups and stews.

3 large shallots, unpeeled
3 large cloves garlic, unpeeled
1 pkg. (12.3 oz. pkg.) silken tofu
1 tsp. purchased beef base
1 tbs. honey

$1/2$ cup light mayonnaise
1 can (8 oz.) water chestnuts, chopped
1 pkg. (10 oz.) frozen spinach, thawed, squeezed dry

Heat oven to 350°. Wrap shallots and garlic in foil and roast for 35 to 45 minutes, until very soft. Peel and chop shallots and garlic; set aside. Drain tofu well and place in a blender container or food processor workbowl. Blend until smooth. Place processed tofu in a bowl. Add beef base, honey, mayonnaise, shallots, garlic and water chestnuts. Mix until well combined. Chop spinach, add to tofu mixture and blend well. Refrigerate for at least 1 hour before serving.

BÉCHAMEL SAUCE

There's no cream here or added fat! With cheese, this sauce is great with cooked vegetables, fish, eggs or pasta. Without cheese, it's perfect in cream soups, casseroles or gravies.

1 cup milk
1 cup (8 oz.) silken tofu
1 bouillon cube, crumbled (any flavor)
$1/4$ cup unbleached flour
$1/2$ cup grated cheddar or Swiss cheese, optional
salt and pepper to taste

In a medium saucepan, blend milk, tofu, bouillon cube and flour until smooth. Cook over medium heat, whisking constantly, until mixture comes to a boil. Reduce heat to low and simmer, whisking, until smooth and thick. Fold in cheese, if using, and salt and pepper. Cook until cheese is melted and sauce has reached desired consistency.

ALTERNATIVE MAYONNAISE

Use this dressing instead of mayonnaise in potato or pasta salads.

1 cup (8 oz.) silken tofu, well drained
1 tbs. Dijon mustard

2 tbs. white wine vinegar
salt and pepper to taste

Process tofu in a food processor workbowl or blender container until smooth. Add mustard, vinegar, salt and pepper and process to combine.

BLUE CHEESE MAYONNAISE

Makes about 1 cup

Blue cheese adds a great tang to dips, salad dressings—and mayonnaise.

1/2 cup *Alternative Mayonnaise,* above
1/4 cup buttermilk
1/4 cup crumbled blue cheese
1 clove garlic, minced

Mix ingredients well in a small bowl. Refrigerate and serve. This recipe can also be made with milk instead of buttermilk.

AVOCADO MAYONNAISE

Use this dressing for sandwiches or salads. Avocadoes are a healthy food, as they are high in unsaturated fat and they contain vitamin C, thiamin and riboflavin.

1/2 avocado, mashed
1 tbs. lemon juice
1 tbs. fresh parsley
1 small clove garlic, minced
1 tbs. capers
1/2 cup *Alternative Mayonnaise,* page 94

Mix all ingredients well in a small bowl immediately before serving.

SESAME SAUCE

Small quantities of seeds can be ground in a spice or coffee mill. Grind larger quantities in a meat grinder or puree in a blender container with ½ teaspoon of oil. When grinding seeds, use a light cycle, so that seeds are well crushed but not oily.

¼ cup sesame seeds
⅓ cup silken tofu
1 tsp. sesame oil

1 tbs. rice vinegar
1½ tbs. soy sauce

Lightly toast sesame seeds in a skillet over medium heat until golden brown. Puree tofu and seeds in a blender container or food processor workbowl. Add oil, vinegar and soy sauce and blend well. Cool and refrigerate. This sauce keeps well for about 7 days.

SESAME DRESSING

Makes ½ cup

¼ cup seasoned rice vinegar
¼ cup fat-free, reduced sodium chicken broth
1 tbs. reduced-sodium soy sauce

1 tbs. sesame oil
1 clove garlic, minced
1 dash hot pepper sauce

Whisk together all ingredients in a small bowl. Refrigerate and serve.

SOYBEAN SPREAD AND DIP

Makes about 2 cups

Substitute cardamom, coriander, chili powder or perhaps grated orange peel for the pepper to vary the flavor of this tasty spread.

1 cup cooked soybeans
½ cup sliced onions
1 clove garlic, minced
½ cup sesame seeds
1–2 tbs. lemon juice
1 pinch pepper

Mash soybeans well with a fork in a bowl. Stir in onions, garlic, sesame seeds, lemon juice and pepper. Mix well to create a thick spread.

TANGY SESAME SOYBEAN SPREAD

Makes about 2 cups

This is a variation of hummus, with soybeans substituting for the chickpeas. Serve with pita wedges, crudités, or as a spread on sandwiches.

1 cup cooked soybeans
1/3 cup tahini (sesame seed paste)
2 tbs. lemon juice
1/3 cup diced onion
1 clove garlic, minced
1 tbs. honey
1 tbs. soy sauce
1 pinch pepper

In a bowl, mash soybeans well with a fork. Add tahini, lemon juice, onion, garlic, honey, soy sauce and pepper and mash together until smooth.

ROASTED ONION AND GARLIC SPREAD

Makes 2 cups

This wonderfully-flavored spread is very low in fat. Garlic and onions both become very sweet and mild when roasted. Serve with sliced baguettes or raw vegetables.

3 large sweet onions, coarsely chopped
10 medium cloves garlic, quartered
2 tbs. olive oil
1 tbs. honey
1/2 cup (4 oz.) silken tofu
salt and pepper to taste

Place onions and garlic in a microwave-safe bowl. Cover and microwave for 8 minutes. Place in a blender container. Add oil, honey, tofu, salt and pepper and blend until smooth.

BLUE CHEESE AND TOFU SPREAD

Serve this tangy spread with crackers, crudités or pita bread wedges.

2 cloves garlic, minced
¹/₂ cup (4 oz.) silken tofu, drained
¹/₄ cup blue cheese, softened
¹/₂ tsp. pepper
1 tbs. fresh lemon juice, or to taste

Combine all ingredients in a food processor workbowl or blender container. Process until smooth. Cover and refrigerate for 30 minutes to allow flavors to blend.

DILL GARLIC SAUCE

This versatile sauce is wonderful on thinly sliced cucumbers or poached fish.

½ cup (4 oz.) silken tofu
½ cup plain low-fat yogurt
2 tbs. lemon juice
2 cloves garlic, minced
2 tbs. chopped fresh dill

Combine all ingredients in a food processor workbowl or blender container and blend until well mixed. Refrigerate for at least 4 hours before serving.

ALTERNATIVE PASTA SAUCE

Servings: 4–6

This sauce has all the texture and flavor of a meat spaghetti sauce, without the cholesterol. Serve over pasta or rice.

4 tsp. olive oil, divided
1½ cups chopped onion
2 cloves garlic, minced
2 stalks celery, chopped
14 oz. TSP (textured soy protein) or tempeh, crumbled
1 cup shredded carrots

1 cup sliced mushrooms
1 can (28 oz.) chopped tomatoes
1 can (15 oz.) tomato sauce
2 tsp. dried basil
1 tsp. dried oregano
1 dash hot pepper sauce
salt to taste

Heat 2 tsp. of the olive oil in a large saucepan over medium heat. Add onion, garlic and celery. Cook until tender. Add remaining 2 tsp. oil and TSP and sauté until browned. Stir in carrots, mushrooms, tomatoes, tomato sauce, basil, oregano, pepper sauce and salt. Simmer for about 20 minutes to allow flavors to blend.

TOFU SALAD DRESSING

As an alternative, try making this versatile dressing without the oil—it's still delicious, and now fat-free!

1 cup (8 oz.) silken tofu
2 tbs. white vinegar
¼ cup olive oil
2 large cloves garlic, minced

1 tbs. Dijon mustard
1 tbs. chopped fresh parsley
salt and pepper to taste

In a small bowl, beat together tofu, vinegar, oil, garlic and mustard. Add parsley, salt and pepper. Refrigerate until ready to serve. The dressing will last 3 days in the refrigerator.

VARIATIONS
¼ cup crumbled blue cheese
1 tbs. capers
½ small avocado, mashed

Add any or all of the above ingredients to the basic salad dressing.

SHOYU DIPPING SAUCES *(TSUKE-JIRU)*

The following preparations are widely used with simmered or deep-fried tofu cubes.

CHINESE STYLE DIPPING SAUCE

Makes ¼ cup

3 tbs. soy sauce
½ tsp. hot mustard
1 tsp. sesame oil
2 tsp. rice wine vinegar

Combine ingredients in a small bowl and mix well.

KOREAN STYLE DIPPING SAUCE

Makes ¼ cup

3 tbs. soy sauce
¾ tsp. sesame oil
¼ tsp. Tabasco Sauce, or 1 pinch dried red pepper flakes
1 tsp. minced garlic

Combine ingredients in a small bowl and mix well.

CARAMEL CORN

Soy nuts are available in the produce department of most supermarkets as well as in health food stores and co-ops. They are sold roasted with or without salt. They make a tasty nutritious snack, especially for children.

3 quarts popped corn
1 cup soy nuts
1 cup brown sugar, packed
1/4 cup light corn syrup

1/2 cup soy margarine
1/4 tsp. salt
1/4 tsp. baking soda
1 tsp. vanilla extract

Place popcorn and soy nuts in a large paper bag; set aside. Mix brown sugar, corn syrup, margarine and salt in a large microwave-safe bowl. Place in microwave, heat on high until boiling, and boil for 2 minutes.

Remove from microwave and stir in baking soda and vanilla. Pour mixture over popcorn and soy nuts in the paper bag. Shake well to combine. Fold over top of bag to seal and place in microwave. Cook on high for 1 minute. Remove bag and shake well. Microwave again for 1 minute; shake and microwave again for 1 minute. Pour onto a cookie sheet and cool. Store in an airtight container.

SPICY ROASTED SOY NUTS

Roasted soy nuts are produced from cleaned, dry, whole beans. In Japan, roasted soybeans are regarded as "beans of good fortune," enjoyed on the first day of the lunar spring.

3 cups whole dried soybeans
2 tsp. salt
1 tsp. garlic powder
2 tsp. chili powder

Soak soybeans overnight in water to cover. Heat oven to 300°. Drain beans well and spread on a lightly oiled cookie sheet. Sprinkle with salt, garlic powder and chili powder. Bake for about 1 hour, shaking pan every 15 minutes, until soybeans are lightly browned.

SPICY TOFU APPETIZERS

Tofu acts like a sponge, soaking up any flavors added to it.

16 oz. firm tofu, sliced $1/2$-inch thick
2 tbs. soy sauce, divided
$1/3$ cup tahini (sesame seed paste)
1 tbs. fresh lemon juice
$1/2$ cup sesame seeds
2 tbs. olive oil

Heat the broiler or grill. Cut each tofu slice into 2 triangles. Brush 1 tbs. of the soy sauce over tofu slices. Set aside. In a small bowl, combine tahini, lemon juice, sesame seeds, oil and remaining 1 tbs. soy sauce. Brush over tofu slices. Broil or grill tofu until golden brown. Serve piping hot.

BREADS

APPLE BREAD

This moist, sweet bread could be called a nutritious cake.

6 apples, peeled
2 tsp. cinnamon
2 cups plus 6 tbs. sugar, divided
3 cups flour
1 tbs. baking powder

1 tsp. salt
4 eggs
1/4 cup unflavored soymilk
2 1/2 tsp. vanilla extract
1/2 pkg. (12.3 oz. pkg.) silken tofu, drained

Heat oven to 350°. Chop apples finely. Sprinkle with cinnamon and 6 tbs. of the sugar and set aside. In a large bowl, mix well flour, baking powder, salt and remaining 2 cups sugar. In another bowl, mix eggs, soymilk, vanilla and tofu. Add tofu mixture to flour mixture and beat until smooth. Spray a tube pan or two 8 x 4-inch loaf pans with nonstick cooking spray. Spread a layer of batter in the prepared pan and top with a layer of apples. Continue layering with remaining apples and batter, ending with batter. Bake for about 90 minutes for tube pan, or 45 to 50 minutes for loaf pan, or until a toothpick inserted in center comes out clean.

BIG BATCH SOY MUFFIN MIX

Makes mix for 4 dozen muffins

Store this muffin mix in the refrigerator for up to 1 month.

8¾ cups all-purpose flour
1¼ cups soy flour
1 cup sugar

¼ cup baking powder
2 tsp. baking soda
2 tsp. salt

Mix together thoroughly all ingredients. Transfer to an airtight container or bag and store in the refrigerator.

FOR EACH BATCH OF 12 MUFFINS

1½ cup unflavored soymilk
1½ cup soy yogurt
¼ cup vegetable oil

2 eggs
2⅔ cups soy muffin mix

Heat oven to 400°. Spray muffin cups with nonstick cooking spray or use paper liners. In a large bowl, stir together soymilk, soy yogurt, oil and eggs until well blended. Add soy muffin mix to liquid mixture. Stir until batter is moistened. Do not overmix.

Divide batter evenly into muffin cups. Bake for 20 to 22 minutes, until toothpick inserted in center of muffin comes out clean. Cool before removing from pan.

CORN MUFFINS

These muffins are the perfect accompaniment to chili: they are also delicious warm, with a little butter.

1 1/2 cups cornmeal
1/2 cup all-purpose flour
1 tsp. sugar
1 tbs. baking powder
1 tsp. ground mild chili powder
1/4 tsp. salt
1 can (8 oz.) creamed corn
2 tbs. vegetable oil
1/4 cup finely chopped green onion
3/4 cup (6 oz.) silken tofu, drained, pureed

Heat oven to 425°. Spray 18 muffin cups with nonstick cooking spray, or use paper liners. In a large bowl, stir together cornmeal, flour, sugar, baking powder, chili powder and salt. Add creamed corn, oil, green onion and tofu. Stir just until combined. Pour into muffin cups. Bake for 15 to 20 minutes. Cool for 10 minutes before serving.

SOY BREAD

Great for sandwiches, this bread is packed with flavor and nutrition.

2 cups unflavored soymilk
$^2/_3$ cup brown sugar, packed
$^1/_3$ cup butter, softened
2 cups soy flour
1 tbs. active dry yeast

$^1/_2$ cup warm water, about 110°
1 egg, beaten
1 tbs. salt
$4^1/_2$–5 cups unbleached flour

In a saucepan over low heat, warm soymilk. Pour into a large bowl and add brown sugar, butter and soy flour. Beat until smooth. In a small bowl, dissolve yeast in warm water. Add yeast mixture, egg, salt and $4^1/_2$ cups of the flour to milk mixture. Knead dough on a lightly floured board for 1 minute, adding more flour if necessary. Divide dough in half.

Shape into 2 loaves. Place in 9 x 5-inch loaf pans, cover and let rise in a warm place until doubled in size.

Heat oven to 375°. Bake for 45 minutes. If loaves become too brown while baking, cover with foil.

PIZZA DOUGH

Why buy frozen pizza when homemade is this easy? Top this chewy crust with your favorite ingredients.

1 tsp. cornmeal
1 tsp. honey
½ cup warm water
1 tbs. active dry yeast (1 pkg.)
1 cup unbleached flour
¼ tsp. salt
¼ cup grated firm tofu
2 tbs. olive oil

Heat oven to 425°. Lightly grease a 12-inch pizza pan and sprinkle with cornmeal. In a small bowl, dissolve honey in warm water. Add yeast and let stand for 10 minutes, or until yeast is bubbly. In a medium bowl, mix flour, salt and tofu. Add yeast and oil. Knead for 6 to 8 minutes, until smooth. Dough will be firm. Roll out dough to fit into prepared pizza pan. To make pizza, add your favorite toppings and bake for about 15 minutes.

BANANA BREAD

This bread is delicious sliced and spread with cream cheese.

1 cup light brown sugar, packed
½ cup (1 stick) butter, softened
½ cup (4 oz.) silken tofu, drained and
   pureed
2 tsp. vanilla extract
2 eggs
2 cups all-purpose flour

1 cup mashed ripe bananas (about 2 large
   bananas)
1 tsp. baking soda
¼ tsp. salt
1 tsp. ground allspice
½ cup chopped nuts, optional

    Heat oven to 350°. Spray a 9 x 5-inch loaf pan with nonstick cooking spray. Beat brown sugar and butter in a medium bowl until light and fluffy. Beat in tofu, vanilla, bananas and eggs until combined. In another bowl, stir together flour, baking soda, salt and allspice. Add flour mixture to banana mixture and stir just until combined. Stir in nuts, if using.

    Pour batter into prepared loaf pan. Bake for about 45 minutes, or until center springs back when lightly pressed. Cool in pan for 10 minutes and turn out on a wire rack to finish cooling.

DRINKS

SOYMILK

You can soak the beans for this recipe during the day while you are at work and make the milk in the evening, allowing it to be fresh and cold the next morning. When cooling, a thick film forms on the milk. Simply skim it off.

1/8 cup soybeans
6 cups water, divided

Put soybeans in a bowl, add 1 cup of the water and soak overnight. In the morning bring 3 cups of the water to a boil in a large saucepan over high heat.

While waiting for the water to boil, pour beans into a colander and rinse well. Place beans in a blender container, add remaining 2 cups water and puree beans. Pour bean mixture into the pot of boiling water. Reduce heat to low and cook gently, uncovered, for 30 minutes. Check frequently as mixture tends to become frothy and spill over. Line a colander with cheesecloth and place colander in a large bowl. Strain soy mixture through lined colander. Discard solids and refrigerate the milk immediately.

EASY SOYMILK

Homemade soymilk can be flavored with sweeteners including vanilla, chocolate, or whatever you prefer.

3 cups water
1 cup full-fat soy flour

Bring water to a boil in a large saucepan over high heat. Slowly pour soy flour into water. Reduce heat and simmer, uncovered, for 20 minutes, stirring occasionally. Line a colander with cheesecloth and place colander in a large bowl. Strain soy mixture through lined colander. Refrigerate the milk immediately.

SESAME SOYMILK FOR CHILDREN

Soymilk is richer than dairy milk in every nutrient except calcium (a mineral essential for babies and growing children). The world's richest source of calcium is the sesame seed, which contains over six times as much calcium by weight as dairy milk. Since soy and sesame proteins complement one another (amino acids low in one are high in the other), their combination makes an abundance of high-quality protein.

1 cup warm unflavored soymilk
1½ tbs. tahini (sesame seed paste)
1½ tsp. honey or sugar
1 pinch salt

Combine all ingredients, mixing well. Serve warm or refrigerate and serve cold.

PINEAPPLE FIX

It is very easy—and very healthy—to make a variety of blender drinks with soymilk and tofu.

½ cup crushed pineapple, frozen
1 tsp. coconut extract or pina colada extract

¾ cup (6 oz.) silken tofu
¼ cup unflavored soymilk

Blend all ingredients in a blender container. Refrigerate until ice cold and serve.

PEACH NECTAR

This is a very smooth and sweet health drink.

3 soft ripe peaches, peeled and sliced
1 carton (8 oz.) peach yogurt
¼ cup raspberries

½ cup unflavored soymilk
2 ice cubes

Puree all ingredients in a blender container and serve immediately.

BANANA MILKSHAKE

3 ice cubes
1/3 cup unflavored soymilk
1/3 cup fat-free vanilla yogurt
1/2 banana
1/4 tsp. vanilla extract
2 tsp. sugar

Puree ice cubes and soymilk in a blender container for 1 minute. Add yogurt, banana, vanilla and sugar and blend for 1 minute. Pour and serve.

ORANGE WHIP

1/2 cup orange juice
1 cup (8 oz.) silken tofu

1 cup carbonated water
orange zest for garnish

Freeze orange juice in an ice cube tray. Puree frozen orange juice cubes, tofu and carbonated water in a blender container. Top with a sprinkling of orange zest.

FRUIT SHAKE

Makes 1

You may wish to substitute your preferred fruits in this shake according to your taste.

2 ice cubes
½ cup (4 oz.) silken tofu
juice of ½ lemon

½ banana
1 cup fresh strawberries
maple syrup to taste

Blend all ingredients in a blender container until smooth. Add a little soymilk if mixture is too thick. Serve immediately.

MANGO ON ICE

Makes 1

Mangoes, which originated in India, are rich in vitamins A, C and D.

¼ cup apple juice
1 mango, peeled, pitted and diced
1 cup carbonated water

juice of ½ lemon
¼ cup (2 oz.) silken tofu

Freeze apple juice in an ice cube tray. Blend frozen juice cubes, mango, carbonated water lemon juice and tofu in a blender container until frothy. Serve immediately.

PEACH FUZZ

Makes 2

Peaches have a particularly juicy and subtle taste which works well in smoothies.

1 ripe peach
8 oz. vanilla low-fat yogurt
1/2 cup unflavored soymilk

1 tbs. brown sugar
1/2 tsp. vanilla
6–8 ice cubes

Peel, pit and quarter peach. In a blender container combine yogurt, peach, soymilk, brown sugar and vanilla. While blender is running, add ice cubes. Blend until smooth. Pour into glasses. Serve immediately.

STRAWBERRY SMOOTHIE

Makes 2–3

1 cup vanilla soymilk
1 cup (8 oz.) silken tofu
1 box (10 oz.) frozen strawberries

1/2 cup orange juice
1 tbs. honey

Place all ingredients in a blender container. Mix on high, until thoroughly blended and mixture is smooth and creamy. Serve immediately or refrigerate.

DESSERTS

RHUBARB STRAWBERRY PIE

Tofu adds a healthy twist to the traditional favorite combination of rhubarb and strawberry flavors.

3 cups cubed fresh or frozen rhubarb,
    thawed
1 cup sliced strawberries
1 cup (8 oz.) silken tofu
1 tbs. vanilla extract
1 cup sugar

1 unbaked piecrust, 9-inch
1/3 cup plus 2 tbs. flour, divided
2 tbs. brown sugar
2 tbs. wheat germ
2 tbs. butter, melted

Heat oven to 350°. Place rhubarb and strawberries in a medium bowl. In a small bowl with a hand blender or mixer, beat tofu and vanilla until smooth. Mix in sugar and 1/3 cup of the flour. Pour mixture over rhubarb and strawberries, stirring gently to coat fruits. Spoon into piecrust.

In a small bowl, combine remaining 2 tbs. flour, brown sugar, wheat germ and butter until crumbly. Sprinkle over pie. Bake for 45 to 50 minutes, or until fruit is tender. Cool to room temperature before serving.

TOFU ORANGE ALMOND DESSERT

Oranges and almonds make another classic flavor combination. This light dessert makes a refreshing finish to any meal.

1 cup fresh orange juice
2 tbs. sugar or honey
1 1/2 tsp. grated orange rind
1/8 tsp. almond extract
1 pkg. (14 oz. pkg.) firm tofu, cut into 1/2 inch cubes
1 cup tangerine sections, syrup drained
3 tbs. toasted almonds

Combine orange juice and sugar in a small saucepan and simmer, uncovered, over medium-low heat until reduced to about 3/4 cup. Stir in orange rind and almond extract. Combine mixture with tofu and tangerine sections in a serving bowl. Cover and chill for at least 2 hours. Serve in dessert cups and top with sliced almonds.

TOFU FRUIT DELIGHT

Any fresh fruit will work well in this beautiful dessert; ripe peaches are especially good.

4 cups low-fat ricotta cheese
1 pkg. (12.3 oz. pkg.) silken tofu, well drained
1 tsp. vanilla extract
3/4 cup sugar, divided
4 boxes (8 cups) small sponge cake pieces
6 cups fresh ripe strawberries

Puree ricotta, tofu, vanilla and 1/2 cup of the sugar in a blender container. Pour into a bowl and set aside. Break sponge cakes into small bite-size pieces. Puree strawberries and remaining 1/4 cup sugar in the blender container. In a deep, clear bowl place a layer of sponge cake; add some strawberry puree and top with a layer of tofu-ricotta mixture. Repeat layers until bowl is filled. Refrigerate until cold.

PINEAPPLE-RUM PARFAIT

If you can't get a fresh pineapple, use 2½ cups unsweetened crushed pineapple, well drained, instead.

1 fresh pineapple, peeled, cored, and cut into ½-inch dice
1 cup coarsely chopped pitted dates
2–3 tbs. honey
juice of 1 large lime
2 tbs. dark rum
1 tsp. vanilla extract
1 pkg. (12.3 oz. pkg.) silken tofu, drained
2–3 tbs. flaked coconut for garnish

Place 1 cup of the pineapple pieces in a food processor workbowl. Refrigerate remaining pineapple. To pineapple in processor, add dates, 2 tbs. of the honey, lime juice, rum and vanilla. Pulse until finely chopped. Add tofu and puree until smooth. If needed, add more honey to taste. Transfer to a covered container and refrigerate. To serve, layer reserved diced pineapple with chilled mixture in individual parfait glasses or bowls, beginning and ending with pineapple. Sprinkle each serving with coconut flakes.

LEMON TORTA WITH GINGERSNAP CRUST

This torta is similar to a lemon cheesecake, without all the fat.

8 oz. gingersnap cookies, broken
1/2 tsp. ground ginger
1/4 cup unsalted butter or margarine, melted
1/2 cup freshly squeezed lemon juice
2 tbs. cornstarch

1/2 tsp. salt
2 pkg. (12.3 oz. pkg.) silken tofu, drained
grated zest of 3 lemons
1/2 cup honey
1 tsp. vanilla extract

Heat oven to 325°. Lightly butter sides of a 9-inch springform pan. In a food processor workbowl or blender container, process cookies and ginger to fine crumbs. Transfer crumbs to a bowl. Add melted butter and combine well. Press crumb mixture evenly into bottom and 1/4 inch up sides of prepared pan. Bake for 10 minutes. Remove pan and set oven at 325°. In a small bowl, whisk lemon juice, cornstarch and salt until dissolved. Puree tofu in a blender container until creamy. Add cornstarch mixture, zest, honey and vanilla. Puree until well blended. Wrap bottom and sides of the pan in heavy foil to prevent leakage. Pour filling into crust. Place springform pan in a larger pan. Place pans in the oven and carefully pour boiling water into larger pan to halfway up sides of springform pan. Bake for 35 minutes. Torta will be jiggly. Remove torta from water bath, remove foil, cool for 1 hour and refrigerate overnight.

SILKEN STRAWBERRY TOPPING

Versatile and super-simple, this topping can be made up to 2 days ahead and served in several ways. Layer it with ice cream and fresh berries; spoon it over pound cake or angel food cake and garnish with fresh berries; or use it as a dressing for a fruit salad.

1 pkg. (12.3 oz. pkg.) silken tofu, drained
¼–½ cup honey
2 tbs. berry-flavored liqueur, such as framboise or creme de cassis, optional
4 cups fresh strawberries, or 1 lb. frozen, partially thawed

In a food processor workbowl or blender container, puree tofu until creamy. Add ¼ cup of the honey and liqueur, if using. Puree until well blended. Add strawberries and puree until smooth. Add more honey, if desired. Cover and refrigerate.

RIGHT WAY CHOCOLATE PIE

Let this recipe be your first bold move into the field of cooking with soy. Each year at the Delaware State Fair I take several of these pies. The children, as they pass, turn up their noses at the thought of any exploration with soy. Then one brave child will try a piece. Before you know it my pies are being devoured by a hoard of delighted youngsters. Make this for your family—you'll see.

1 pkg. (12 oz. pkg.) semisweet chocolate chips
2 tbs. honey
1 pkg. (14 oz. pkg.) firm tofu, drained
1 graham cracker piecrust
whipped topping for garnish

Melt chocolate chips in microwave or over double boiler. Place honey, tofu and melted chocolate in a blender container or food processor workbowl and puree until smooth. Pour into graham cracker crust. Refrigerate for 4 to 5 hours. Serve with whipped topping.

CHOCOLATE-ORANGE MOUSSE

Oranges and chocolate combine for an elegant dessert.

8 oz. bittersweet chocolate
2 pkg. (12.3 oz. pkg.) silken tofu, drained
½ cup orange marmalade
zest of 1 orange
2 tbs. freshly squeezed orange juice
2 tbs. orange-flavored liqueur, such as Triple Sec
1 tsp. vanilla extract

Chop chocolate into small pieces. Melt chocolate in a microwave or a double boiler. In a food processor workbowl or blender container, puree tofu until creamy, about 30 seconds. Add marmalade, zest, juice, liqueur and vanilla. Puree until smooth. Add melted chocolate and puree until well blended, scraping down sides as needed. Transfer to individual serving dishes and refrigerate.

CHOCOLATE-RASPBERRY TRIFLE

Servings: 8–10

Any soft fresh fruit will work in this versatile dish; try peaches, strawberries, or even bananas with equally delicious results. Use frozen berries in a pinch.

3 cups fresh raspberries
7 oz. ladyfingers
3/4 cup cream sherry
4 oz. bittersweet or semisweet chocolate
1 pkg. (12.3 oz. pkg.) silken tofu, drained

1/2 cup chocolate syrup
1/2 cup raspberry jam or preserves
2 tsp. vanilla extract, divided
1 cup heavy cream
2 tsp. sugar

Set aside a few berries for garnish. Lay ladyfingers in a single layer on a cookie sheet. Sprinkle with sherry, cover pan with plastic wrap and set aside. Melt chocolate in a microwave or a double boiler. In a food processor workbowl or blender container, puree tofu until creamy. Add syrup, jam and 1 tsp. of the vanilla. Puree until smooth. Add melted chocolate and puree until well blended. In a deep glass serving bowl, layer 1/3 of the ladyfingers, 1/3 of the chocolate mixture and 1/2 of the raspberries. (Break some of the ladyfingers in half, if necessary, to fit bowl.) Repeat layers, ending with chocolate mixture, smoothing evenly. Whip cream with sugar and remaining 1 tsp. vanilla to soft peaks. Spread over top of trifle and decorate with reserved berries. Serve immediately.

PUMPKIN PIE

This all-season pie is quick and easy—and remember that pumpkin pie need not be served only on holidays such as Thanksgiving and Christmas. Pumpkin is rich in beta carotene.

1 can (30 oz.) seasoned pumpkin pie filling
2 eggs, or 2 egg whites
1 pkg. (14 oz. pkg.) firm tofu
1 unbaked deep-dish piecrust

Heat oven to 410°. Mix pumpkin, eggs and tofu well in a food processor workbowl or blender container. Pour into piecrust. Bake for 10 minutes, reduce heat to 375° and bake for about 50 minutes, until firm.

DELICIOUSLY LOW-FAT PECAN PIE

Serve this pie with Tofu Whipped Cream, *page 144 or* Tofu Ice Cream, *page 140.*

1/4 tsp. salt

1 1/2 cups plus 3 tbs. all-purpose flour, divided

1/2 cup (1 stick) butter or margarine, chilled, divided

about 1/4 cup water

1 pkg. (12.3 oz. pkg.) silken tofu, drained

1/2 cup pure maple syrup

1/2 cup nonfat condensed milk

1 tbs. vanilla extract

1 1/2 cups pecan halves

Combine salt and 1 1/2 cups of the flour in a food processor workbowl. Add 1/4 cup of the butter and process until mixture resembles coarse crumbs. Add remaining butter and process until butter is the size of small peas. Add water 1 tbs. at a time, until mixture holds together and can be formed into a ball. Cover with plastic wrap and refrigerate for 30 minutes.

Heat oven to 350°. Roll out dough on a lightly floured board to an 11-inch circle. Fit circle into a 9-inch pie pan. Fold edges under and flute. Set aside. Process tofu and maple syrup in a food processor workbowl until combined. Add condensed milk, remaining 3 tbs. flour and vanilla. Process until smooth. Stir in pecans. Pour filling into crust. Bake for about 40 minutes, or until filling is set. Refrigerate until chilled. Refrigerate leftovers.

CHOCOLATE CAKE

Hidden in each of us is the capability to create things far greater than we ever dreamed of—like making a fat-free, cholesterol-free chocolate cake.

1½ cups unbleached flour
3 tbs. unsweetened cocoa powder
1 tsp. baking soda
1 tsp. baking powder
1 cup sugar

1 tsp. vinegar
1 tsp. vanilla extract
3 tbs. soy oil
½ cup (4 oz.) silken tofu
½ cup warm water

Heat oven to 350°. Grease and flour an 8 x 8-inch baking pan. Sift flour, cocoa, baking soda and baking powder into a large bowl. Add sugar and mix well. In a small bowl, combine vinegar, vanilla, oil, tofu and water. Add to dry ingredients and mix well. Pour into prepared pan. Bake for 35 to 40 minutes, until a toothpick inserted in the center comes out clean.

PIE PASTRY

A light, flaky crust is yours every time with this recipe.

2 cups unbleached flour
1 tsp. baking powder
1/4 tsp. salt
1/2 cup (1 stick) butter, cold
1/4 cup grated firm tofu
1/4 cup ice-cold water

In a medium bowl, combine flour, baking powder and salt. Cut in butter with a pastry blender container. When mixture resembles coarse crumbs, mix in grated tofu. Add water 1 tbs. at a time, until mixture holds together (you may have to adjust amount of water depending upon amount of moisture in tofu). Divide dough in half. Roll dough out on a lightly floured board or on waxed paper. Use half for 1 piecrust. Wrap and freeze the second portion if not needed.

PUMPKIN MOUSSE

Vegetarians can substitute arrowroot for the unflavored gelatin in this recipe.

1 cup apple juice
3/4 cup dark brown sugar
1 envelope (1 tbs.) unflavored gelatin
1 can (15 oz.) unseasoned pumpkin puree
1 tsp. cinnamon
1/2 tsp. ground cloves
1/2 tsp. ground allspice
1 pkg. (14 oz. pkg.) firm tofu
6 tbs. chopped pecans

Stir together apple juice and brown sugar in a small saucepan. Sprinkle gelatin over juice. Warm over low heat, stirring until gelatin is completely dissolved. Set aside.

Puree pumpkin, cinnamon, cloves, allspice and tofu in a food processor workbowl or blender container, until well combined. Add gelatin mixture and process until smooth. Pour pumpkin mixture into 6 parfait glasses. Sprinkle with pecans, cover and refrigerate for 3 hours, or until firm.

PEANUT BUTTER COOKIES

These healthy treats will be a welcome addition to any lunchbox.

3 pkg. (14 oz. pkg.) firm tofu
½ cup peanut butter
¼ cup brown sugar, packed
¼ cup (½ stick) butter, softened
1 egg, lightly beaten
¼ tsp. salt

Heat oven to 350°. In a large bowl, combine tofu, peanut butter, brown sugar, butter, egg and salt, mixing well to form a smooth dough. Shape into small balls. Place balls on an oiled cookie sheet. Press each ball flat with a fork. Bake for 15 minutes. Cool and serve.

TOFU BROWN RICE COOKIES

Similar to oatmeal-raisin cookies, these very healthy cookies are chewy and delicious.

1 pkg. (14 oz. pkg.) firm tofu
1 cup cooked brown rice
3 tbs. sugar, or more to taste
1 tbs. honey
$1/4$ cup raisins
cinnamon
$1/4$ cup shredded coconut

Heat oven to 350°. Blot tofu well with paper towels. Combine tofu, rice, sugar, honey and raisins in a large bowl and mix well. Shape into small patties and arrange on a lightly oiled cookie sheet. Sprinkle with cinnamon and coconut. Bake for 15 to 20 minutes, until browned.

TOFU ICE CREAM

This creamy treat can be enhanced with the addition of nuts, coconut, chopped fruit, chocolate—the variations are endless.

2$\frac{1}{4}$ cups (18 oz.) silken tofu, well chilled, divided
3 tbs. honey
$\frac{1}{4}$ tsp. vanilla extract
$\frac{1}{8}$ tsp. salt

Combine 12 oz. of the tofu, honey, vanilla and salt in a blender container. Puree until smooth. Transfer to a covered container and place in the freezer overnight.

Puree remaining 6 oz. tofu in the blender container until smooth. Cut frozen tofu-honey mixture into small chunks. Add a few chunks at a time to blender container with pureed tofu and blend until all of frozen tofu mixture is incorporated and ice cream is smooth. Serve immediately.

MANGO-TANGELO FREEZE

Use about 24 ounces of frozen mango chunks, partially thawed, if fresh mangos are unavailable. The mango mixture should taste slightly too sweet, as freezing mutes flavors.

3 medium mangoes
6 oz. silken tofu, drained
$1/4$–$1/2$ cup honey, or to taste
juice of 1 medium tangelo or orange, about 3–4 tbs.
1 tsp. vanilla extract
1 pinch salt

Peel and seed mangoes and cut flesh into chunks; set aside. Place tofu in a food processor workbowl or blender container. Puree until creamy. Add $1/4$ cup of the honey, tangelo juice, vanilla and salt. Puree until blended. Add mangoes and puree until smooth. If needed, add more honey to taste. Cover and refrigerate for several hours or overnight.

Freeze in an ice-cream maker according to manufacturer's instructions. Serve immediately or transfer to a covered container and keep frozen. Let stand at room temperature for 20 to 30 minutes to soften before serving.

VANILLA PUDDING

As a child, I fondly remember laying propped with pillows in bed, my face ruddy with the measles, being encouraged to just try a bit of vanilla pudding to regain my strength. Indeed it did just that! You may use sweetened vanilla soymilk in this recipe; if so, there will be no need for the sugar or vanilla.

$1/2$ cup sugar
2 tbs. cornstarch
$1/8$ tsp. salt
$1^1/_2$ cups unflavored soymilk
1 tsp. vanilla extract

In a saucepan, stir together sugar, cornstarch and salt. Slowly add soymilk, stirring to prevent lumps from forming. Place over medium-high heat and bring mixture to a boil. Lower to a simmer and cook, stirring constantly, for about 5 minutes, until mixture is creamy and thick. Remove from heat, stir in vanilla and pour into dessert cups. Chill until set.

TOFU RICE PUDDING

Rice pudding, the ultimate comfort food, gets a nutritious boost from tofu and brown rice. Try substituting dried cherries or apricots for the raisins for a delicious twist.

1 pkg. (14 oz. pkg.) firm tofu, mashed
1 cup cooked brown rice
1 cup unflavored soymilk
3 tbs. honey
1/4 tsp. salt
1/4 tsp. cinnamon
1/4 cup raisins
3 tbs. crushed cornflakes
2 tbs. butter

Heat oven to 350°. Lightly oil a casserole dish. Combine tofu, rice, soymilk, honey, salt and raisins in a large bowl. Mix well. Spoon the tofu/rice mixture into prepared casserole dish, sprinkle with cornflakes and dot with butter. Bake for 25 minutes, or until set. Cool and serve.

TOFU WHIPPED CREAM

This is delicious over strawberries, thinly sliced apples, bananas, pears, peaches or melons. Use silken or firm tofu in this recipe, according to your preference.

12 oz. tofu (silken or firm)
2 tbs. honey or sugar

1/2 tsp. vanilla extract

Combine all ingredients in a blender container or food processor workbowl and puree until smooth.

TOFU CUSTARD PUDDING

1 pkg. (14 oz. pkg.) firm tofu
1 egg
2–2 1/2 tbs. honey

1/2 tsp. salt
1/2 tsp. vanilla extract
1/2 cup *Tofu Whipped Cream,* page 144

Heat oven to 325°. Combine tofu, egg, honey, salt, vanilla and *Tofu Whipped Cream* in a blender container and puree until smooth. Spoon mixture into 3 custard cups. Place cups in a pan of hot water and bake for about 20 minutes. Serve hot or cold.

TOFU STRAWBERRY DESSERT

Perfect for company, this delicious dessert can be prepared well ahead of time. Try raspberries or blueberries in place of the strawberries.

24 oz. silken tofu, chilled and mashed
4½ tbs. honey
2 tsp. vanilla extract
12–15 strawberries, cut vertically in halves
¼ cup sliced hazelnuts or almonds

Mix tofu, honey and vanilla in a food processor workbowl or blender container and puree until smooth. Spoon into dessert glasses. Top with strawberries and then with nuts.

CARROT CAKE

Moist and flavorful, this cake has much less oil than the standard carrot cake.

1 cup unbleached flour
1 cup whole wheat flour
1 1/2 cups brown sugar, packed
2 tsp. baking soda
2 tsp. baking powder
2 tsp. cinnamon
1/2 tsp. ground cloves
3 eggs

1 tsp. vanilla
1/3 cup soy oil
1/2 cup (4 oz.) silken tofu
3 cups grated carrots
1/2 cup grated firm tofu
1/4 cup raisins or dried cranberries
3/4 cup chopped pecans

Heat oven to 350°. Grease two 8 x 4-inch loaf pans. In a large bowl, mix together unbleached and wheat flours, brown sugar, baking powder, baking soda, cinnamon and cloves. In a separate bowl, whisk together eggs, vanilla, oil and silken tofu. Add this mixture to dry ingredients and mix well. Add carrots, firm tofu, raisins and pecans. Mix well. Fill prepared loaf pans. Bake for about 45 minutes, or until a toothpick inserted in the center comes out clean.

CHOCOLATE MOUSSE

A rich chocolate mousse with very little fat? Try it and believe!

1/4 cup semisweet chocolate chips, melted
1 pkg. (14 oz. pkg.) firm tofu
1/4 tsp. salt
3 large egg whites
1/2 cup brown sugar, packed
1/4 cup unflavored soymilk
Tofu Whipped Cream, page 144, for garnish
grated chocolate for garnish

Place chocolate and tofu in a food processor workbowl or blender container. Process for 2 minutes, or until smooth. Beat salt and egg whites in a medium bowl until stiff peaks form. Place brown sugar and soymilk in a saucepan and bring to a boil over high heat. Cook, without stirring, until a candy thermometer registers 238°. Pour hot syrup in a stream over egg whites, beating at high speed. Gently fold in chocolate-tofu mixture. Scoop 1/2 cup of the mousse into eight 6-ounce custard cups. Cover and chill for at least 4 hours. Garnish with *Tofu Whipped Cream* and grated chocolate.

NO-BAKE LEMON CHEESECAKE

Servings: 8

Sweetened condensed milk can be used (omitting sugar). However, I find using plain condensed milk and 1/2–3/4 cup sugar—depending on your sweet tooth—gives a better flavor to the cheesecake.

8 oz. ricotta cheese
1 cup (8 oz.) silken tofu
1 1/2 tsp. vanilla extract
1 can (14 oz. pkg.) condensed milk
3/4 cup sugar
1/2 cup lemon juice
2 tsp. unflavored gelatin
1 graham cracker piecrust, 9-inch

In a blender container, puree ricotta cheese and tofu until smooth. Pour into a bowl and gradually stir in vanilla, condensed milk and sugar. Pour lemon juice into a small saucepan. Sprinkle gelatin over juice. Warm over low heat, stirring occasionally, until gelatin is dissolved. Fold into cheese mixture. Pour into piecrust. Cover and chill for at least 4 hours.

MOCHA MOUSSE

Use real maple syrup for the best flavor in this mousse.

1 pkg. (12 oz.) semisweet chocolate chips
1/4 cup maple syrup
1 pkg. (14 oz. pkg.) firm tofu, drained
1 pkg. (8 oz.) low-fat cream cheese, softened
1 tbs. instant espresso powder dissolved in 2 tbs. hot water
1 tbs. vanilla extract
whipped cream for garnish

Melt chocolate chips with maple syrup in a double boiler, stirring occasionally. Combine tofu and cream cheese in a food processor workbowl and puree until smooth. Add chocolate mixture, coffee and vanilla. Puree until thoroughly combined. Pour into 6 parfait glasses. Refrigerate until firm. Top with whipped cream.

MARBLED TOFU AND BANANA DELIGHT

Try a slice of this unusual loaf for a healthy snack or even breakfast, as well as dessert.

2 pkg. (14 oz. pkg.) firm tofu, crumbled
3 bananas, mashed
$1/2$ cup chopped walnuts
1 pinch nutmeg
$1/4$ tsp. salt

Heat oven to 350°. Grease an 8 x 4-inch loaf pan. Combine tofu, bananas, walnuts, nutmeg and salt in a large bowl and mash together. Press mixture into prepared loaf pan. Bake for 20 to 30 minutes, until lightly browned. Cool before serving.

INDEX

Serve Creative, Easy, Nutritious Meals with nitty gritty® Cookbooks

100 Dynamite Desserts
The 9 x 13 Pan Cookbook
The Barbecue Cookbook
Beer and Good Food
Best Bagels are Made at Home
Best Pizza is Made at Home
Big Book of Bread Machine Recipes
Big Book of Kitchen Appliance Recipes
Big Book of Snacks & Appetizers
Blender Drinks
Bread Baking
Bread Machine Cookbook
Bread Machine Cookbook II
Bread Machine Cookbook III
Bread Machine Cookbook V
Bread Machine Cookbook VI
The Little Burger Bible
Cappuccino/Espresso
Casseroles
The Coffee and Tea Cookbook
Convection Oven Cookery
The Cook-Ahead Cookbook
Cooking for 1 or 2

Cooking in Clay
Cooking on the Indoor Grill
Cooking in Porcelain
Cooking with Chile Peppers
Cooking with Grains
Cooking with Your Kids
New Recipes for your Deep Fryer
The Dehydrator Cookbook
Edible Pockets for Every Meal
Entrees from Your Bread Machine
Extra-Special Crockery Pot Recipes
Fabulous Fiber Cookery
Fondue and Hot Dips
Fresh Vegetables
From Freezer, 'Fridge and Pantry
The Garlic Cookbook
Healthy Cooking on the Run
Healthy Snacks for Kids
From Your Ice Cream Maker
The Juicer Book
The Juicer Book II
Lowfat American Favorites
New International Fondue Cookbook

No Salt, No Sugar, No Fat
One-Dish Meals
The Pasta Machine Cookbook
Pinch of Time: Meals in Less than 30
    Minutes
Quick and Easy Low-Carb Recipes
Quick and Easy Pasta Recipes
Quick and Easy Soy and Tofu Recipes
Recipes for the Loaf Pan
Recipes for the Pressure Cooker
Rotisserie Oven Cooking
New Recipes for Your Sandwich Maker
The Sensational Skillet: Sautés and Stir-Fries
Slow Cooking in Crock-Pot,® Slow Cooker,
    Oven and Multi-Cooker
Simple Substitutions Cookbook
Soups and Stews
Tapas Fantasticas
The Toaster Oven Cookbook
Unbeatable Chicken Recipes
The Vegetarian Slow Cooker
New Waffles and Pizzelles
Wraps and Roll-Ups

For a free catalog, call: **Bristol Publishing Enterprises.**
(800) 346-4889
www.bristolpublishing.com